BEER BREAKS

CAMRA'S POCKET GUIDE TO SOME OF EUROPE'S BEST BEER DESTINATIONS

TIM WEBB

Published by the Campaign for Real Ale Ltd
230 Hatfield Road, St Albans, Hertfordshire AL1 4LW
www.camra.org.uk/books

Text © Tim Webb
Design and layout © Campaign for Real Ale Ltd. 2022
The author's rights have been asserted
This First Edition published in 2022

All rights reserved.
No part of this publication may be reproduced, stored in a retrieval system or transmitted in any form or by any means – electronic, mechanical, photocopying, recording or otherwise – without the prior permission of the Campaign for Real Ale Ltd.

ISBN 978-1-85249-364-6

A CIP catalogue record for this book is available from the British Library

Printed and bound in the United Kingdom by
The Pensord Group, UK

www.carbonbalancedpaper.com
CBP006075

Managing Editor: Alan Murphy
Project Editor: Yvette Caster
Design/typography: Hannah Moore
Sales & Marketing: Toby Langdon
Cover: Jack Pemberton

PHOTO CREDITS
The publisher would like to thank all the bars, cafés, taprooms, bottle shops, tourist offices and others who kindly granted permission for their photography to be used in this book.

Every effort has been made to ensure the contents of this book are correct at the time of printing. Nevertheless, the Publisher cannot be held responsible for any errors or omissions, or for changes in the details given in this book, or for the consequences of any reliance on information provided by the same.
This does not affect your statutory rights.

HOW TO USE THIS BOOK

THE DESTINATIONS

Where local breweries and beer styles are mentioned, these are intended only to add background. They are not essential to understanding the local beer scene. I have prioritised train and, where relevant, ferry connections ahead of local airport links for their lower environmental impact, better travelling experience and allowing the traveller time to reflect.

THE VENUES

COVID caused major disruption to the brewing and hospitality industries all over Europe. Going to press I am reasonably confident that most of the venues chosen will survive the next few years. However, what opening hours they will choose is anyone's guess, so I have included their website or Facebook page, for checking before you visit. Even in normal times, the idea of fixed opening hours is very British.

I have also tried to indicate the nearest metro, tram or bus stop, though where a venue is sited in a pedestrian area, or the connections are too numerous, this may not appear. Most of your phones will be more reliable.

The types of beer venue chosen have been defined using a simple set of symbols:

 A bar/taphouse where little or no food is available

 A bar/taphouse where some food is available

 A restaurant that offers a good beer selection

 A place where beer can be bought to take away

Where the venue supports more than one type of facility the primary one is listed first.

NEED TO KNOW

For accommodation I have assumed you will have a favourite booking website(s) for picking hotels and apartments, so have restricted most comments to recommending areas in which to stay.

For getting around I have been quite directive. Metro and urban train systems, tram and bus networks vary from city to city in how useful they are for people visiting the city, with most designed first and foremost for the locals. The networks I have emphasised are the ones that are most tourist friendly.

Prices given in the book are correct at the time of going to press (Spring 2022).

Exchange rates are also correct at the time of going to press, but for more up-to-date rates check out xe.com.

A little dedication

For Steve and Lesly Plumridge, the long-serving editorial team behind Pints West in Bristol, holders of more CAMRA awards than can fit on any modern mantelpiece, who kindly agreed to host the column on which this book is based.

With special thanks to Jim Cornish, Judith Boyle, Estelle Durand, Andreas Fält and Shacha Hertz, without whom this book and I would have been a lot shakier.

CONTENTS

- 6   Introduction
- 8   Getting to and around Europe
- 14   Brewing traditions and beer styles
- 20   How to drink beer
- 24   What to eat
- 30   The European beer events calendar
- 34   The price of beer in Europe

BEER DESTINATIONS

36	Amsterdam	106	Ljubljana
42	Antwerp	110	Luxembourg
46	Athens	112	Madrid
48	Bamberg	116	Oslo
52	Barcelona	120	Paris
56	Berlin	124	Porto
62	Bologna	126	Prague
66	Bordeaux	132	Reykjavík
70	Bristol	136	Riga
74	Brussels	140	Rome
80	Budapest	144	Stockholm
84	Copenhagen	148	Tallinn
88	Dublin	152	Tel Aviv
92	Edinburgh	156	Vienna
96	Gibraltar	160	Wrocław
98	Hamburg		
102	Helsinki	164	Index

INTRODUCTION

Having to put the finishing touches to a book about how to travel around Europe in pursuit of great beer at a time when I was barred from traveling much beyond the end of my street felt a bit odd. Before COVID broke in spring 2020 I had got used to spending a lot of time drifting from country to country, with beer as my excuse.

COVID delayed this book by two years and necessitated a thorough rewrite, to account for the damage inflicted by the virus and more significantly by the restrictions it spawned. The updates brought a heady mix of sadness for those pubs, bars and cafés that did not make it through, and delight at those that have survived.

Travel is now less trivial than before COVID. Crossing borders involves more regulation, to counter fear of disease, and, for we British, as a result of the decision to leave the EU. Attitudes to travel are also having to adapt to meeting a greater challenge, to mitigate climate change so that our descendants may survive.

The first global pandemic of the internet age has likely taught us something about coping, though we have known worse, of course.

In 1950 my recently married parents travelled to Switzerland for a short foreign holiday, a new experience for each of them. They flew on a converted Dakota troop carrier that, only five or six years earlier, had probably taken soldiers to fight in the various countries over which they were now flying. It was they who taught my sisters and I that to understand the world we must explore and experience it, and that if we fail to do so, we limit ourselves.

My mother died during the writing of this book, not from COVID but because her well-spent time came to its natural end. She never liked beer. She said it smelled funny, so that was that. While she never understood why I would drink it, even she could spot that its nature and ambitions had changed beyond all recognition in the past few decades.

So, with apologies for the slight delay, I now invite you to explore and experience a trail that might take you to sharing Imperial Stout from ice buckets on the Costa Brava, a hop-free rye beer from the Finnish lakes that tastes of cake, and some authentic 17th century style lagers in a UNESCO World Heritage Site. Why? For no better reason than to begin celebrating living once more.

Tim Webb,
Devon, UK, April 2022

GETTING TO AND AROUND EUROPE

The modern traveller uses three forms of currency: money, time and environmental impact. As with making beer, there is no correct way to travel, it's just a question of different options and how you cost them.

PLANNING THE TRIP

Finishing work at lunchtime on Friday and heading off to the airport; fretting in the queue and getting frustrated by small delays; arriving at your destination late and settling for necking a few average beers in triple time in the wrong bar; having to squeeze more places into Saturday and drinking too much; feeling battered on Sunday morning and tolerating lunch, before hitting the Sunday evening airport queues for a regular Monday start is not a great travel experience.

So, whenever possible, stretch your timetable a little. Take the slower route. Sift the must-dos from the might-dos. Enjoy the journey as much as the destination. Turn a bash into an experience; you will love it far more.

COVID, Brexit and the need to tackle climate change have all made flying off for a boozy weekend on the Continent more difficult, so maybe string a few trips together and put in some real exploring along the way, or for those now able to work online, try a new type of working holiday.

BY RAIL

The equation that weighs up comfort, value, speed and environmental impact will usually end with the answer that your best option for exploring Europe is to take the train. It is a lot less faff than flying, has fewer hidden costs and offers more room to stretch, read, work and so on. The views are better too.

For straightforward scheduling advice try **raileurope.com** or **thetrainline.com**.

Trains between the UK and Europe

The only direct train links from the UK to mainland Europe go through the Channel Tunnel. The London terminal is St Pancras, though some trains also stop at Ebbsfleet, just off the M25, and occasional ones at Ashford International. Its mainland European destinations are Brussels Midi, Paris Nord, Rotterdam Centraal and Amsterdam Centraal, all of which have onward HST connections. Most stop at Lille Europe and a few at Calais Fréthun.

Whenever possible, stretch your timetable a little. Take the slower route

Because of security concerns in the Channel Tunnel the check-in time for Eurostar is quite lengthy, unlike with most other HST services.

Interrail and Eurail Passes

If you are intending to travel on four or more days within as many weeks, or to make multiple trips within a year, then seriously consider buying an Interrail Pass (interrail.eu) or, if you live outside Europe, a Eurail Pass (eurail.com). Interrail and Eurail Passes enable free travel on most of Europe's trains.

What the passes cover

High speed trains (HSTs), regular services and local lines are all included, as are most overnight services and a surprising number of international ferry crossings.

Journeys within the country where you live are only included if en route to an international crossing where you will use a train on the other side, the same rule applying to your return. For the UK, this covers most ferry crossings.

Not included yet are trains in Belarus, Moldova, Ukraine, Albania, or any part of Russia. Also, Iceland has no train system.

Paying for extras

Many HSTs and most overnight trains require advance reservations, usually for

SEAT61.COM

The Man in Seat 61 is Mark Smith, a former railways manager and someone in whom a passion for trains, and for travel more generally, is hardwired. For a website packed with reliable, useful and up-to-date factual information, inspiring suggestions for great journeys, and a sense of being treated like a proper mate, seat61.com is second to none.

USEFUL ADVICE

With a pass there is rarely a need to book too far in advance, except on Eurostar. That said, my advice is that after finalising your itinerary, you make as many bookings as possible in a single go. The booking system for tickets and reservations is not always intuitive, but starts to make sense after a while, and you can always add journeys later. For straightforward scheduling advice try raileurope.com or the trainline.com.

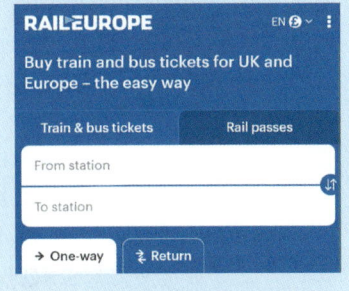

a small fee, occasionally larger. The cost of this is not covered by the pass. Some operators also charge for optional seat reservations, to cover the (usually small) risk of having to stand if every seat is taken. Some trains also offer higher levels of service for a fee.

Booking a journey

Go online to buy your pass, then book the individual journeys. Tickets are sold directly by Interrail (interrail.eu) or Eurail (eurail.com), though any specific reservation is made directly from individual train companies.

Choosing your pass

Passes are either Standard Class or First Class. First Class costs roughly one-third extra and will cover Standard Class tickets on a train that has no First Class compartment. A Standard Class Pass will get you onto the same trains but not into a First Class seat.

On some trains the difference in quality between First and Standard class is negligible, amounting to little more than travelling among people who can afford and choose to buy expensive tickets. On other trains the difference can be huge, a typical deal including wider and more comfortable seats, extra legroom, some complimentary food and drink, and better wi-fi.

The age groups are Adult (aged 28 to 59 on the day of first departure), with substantial discounts for a Senior (60+), Youth (12-27), or accompanied Child (4-11). Children aged under four travel for free but do not always get their own seat.

Passes can cover any four, five or seven days within one month (e.g. 21 March to 20 April), 10 or 15 days in two successive months, or a single continuous period of 15 or 22 days over one, two, or three months. They can be individual or for any number up to 15 people, though there are no savings for larger groups.

GETTING TO AND AROUND EUROPE

BY SEA

One of the most relaxing and enjoyable ways to travel between Europe's many maritime nations is a passenger or car ferry. When exploring Scandinavia and the Baltic rim, these are often the cheapest way of making sometimes unexpected and otherwise complex connections.

From the UK, overnight services with hotel standards run between Hull and Rotterdam or Zeebrugge, Newcastle and Ijmuiden (for Amsterdam), and Portsmouth or Plymouth and northern Spain, making holiday experiences in their own right. This is mirrored on routes across the Mediterranean between Spain and Italy, the viability of which is maintained by the cost of tolls on roads between the two.

For the most adventurous, I recommend Smyril Lines' route from Hirtshal in Denmark, via the Faroe Islands, to the east coast of Iceland at Seyðisfjörður.

BY AIR

The network of short-haul flights within Europe, along with their timetables, was blown apart by the reaction to COVID. That said, even before then the changes to airports, routes and carriers were so rapid that even the most assiduous websites failed to hold a majority of the options.

Most European countries have a plethora of local airports offering all the advantages and disadvantages of being small – better parking, less people, fewer facilities, not so many destinations. An equally unpredictable cluster of airlines operate, offering fares that look temptingly low until you factor in the cost of luggage and legroom, plus fines for not checking in electronically before your flight.

Calculating the length of a flight is not straightforward either, if you factor in the time it takes to check in and the journeys to and from airports. I have

tried to include a user-friendly guide to the latter, borne of the untold weeping that resulted from having taken the longer, more expensive route, the pointless taxi, the coach that goes via another city, or the train that is not the metro.

After forty years of travelling round Europe it's not climate change that sees me most often on trains – it's the increasing tedium of flying.

From outside Europe

For those coming from North America or elsewhere the four biggest hubs for direct long-haul flights are London Heathrow, Paris Charles de Gaulle, Frankfurt, and Amsterdam Schiphol. Of these, the one with the best onward connections is Schiphol, both by air and train.

Two other hubs worth considering are Dublin (Ireland), from which return flights to the US enjoy a border crossing on site, and Reykjavík (Iceland), routing through which involves two shorter haul flights, with an option of a side-trip to this unique land.

BY ROAD

Of course, you can drive yourself around Europe, though be aware that the drink driving regulations are generally tougher than the UK's constricting 80 milligrams per litre (mg/l). Most other European nations hold to a tighter 50 mg/l, while Norway, Sweden, Estonia and Poland impose a stifling 20 mg/l, and the Czech Republic, Slovak Republic and Hungary expect zero, which means in theory that drinking alcohol within twelve hours of getting behind the wheel is unwise.

There are also some unexpected expenses that can be predicted to rise as climate change mitigation gets serious. Tolls on faster roads are common in France, Italy, Spain, Greece and Portugal and also appear elsewhere, while Austria, the Czech Republic, Hungary, Slovakia, Slovenia and Switzerland all require vignettes, a spot purchase form of road tax, for otherwise free use of them for a year.

Additionally, be aware that winter tyres and/or snow chains are mandatory in many parts of northern and central Europe at times between November and April.

TAKING THE BUS

I have not noted details about long-distance buses, as the options are so broad. They really come into their own in the Baltic States, where the trains are few and far between, and Iceland, which has none, but are also viable alternatives between most other places.

Leading trans-European operators include BlaBlaBus, Eurolines, FlixBus, Irish Citylink, Megabus and National Express, all of which can be researched and booked through the comparison site **comparabus.com**.

BREWING TRADITIONS AND BEER STYLES

There is no correct way to make a beer. Its alcohol content, intensity, flavours, colour, bitterness and carbonation, even the extent of its foam, are all determined by preference, circumstances and technique.

Describing a type of beer by its colour, strength and method of production has occurred in different ways across Europe for centuries. Dividing beers by 'style' is a newer idea, tracing its origins to beer writer Michael Jackson, who in his *World Guide to Beer* and other ground-breaking publications of the late 20th century, chose to describe diverse types of beer by the names they had accrued in different cultures.

In that book's successor, *The World Atlas of Beer*, which I write with Canadian beer writer Stephen Beaumont, we said: 'A beer style is as an informal agreement between a brewer and a customer, expressed through a term on a label, by which the former tells the latter roughly what sort of beer they aimed to make.'

The purpose of stylising beers is not to limit a brewer's options – an unclassifiable beer can be every bit as good as a classic of its kind – but rather to minimise the times a consumer has to pay for a misunderstanding.

STYLE CLASSIFICATION SYSTEMS

What follows here is an outline of the main styles of European beer that you will likely encounter on your travels. For greater detail, three near-comprehensive classification systems for beer styles worth taking a longer look at are the European Beer Consumers Union (EBCU) *Beer Styles of Europe and Beyond* (ebcu.org), compiled from the consumer perspective, the *Beer Judge Certification Program (BJCP)* guidelines for judges in beer competitions, and the Brewers Association (BA) *Beer Style Guidelines* for North American brewers. In largest part, these describe the same range from different perspectives.

AUTHENTIC LAGERS

The crucial difference between ales and lagers is the yeast used to ferment them. Ale yeast strains add volatile,

> *The purpose of stylising beers is not to limit a brewer's options but rather to minimise the times a consumer has to pay for a misunderstanding.*

slightly fruity flavours during fermentation, while lager yeast strains do not, the beer's flavour coming mostly from the other ingredients and how they are handled.

Industrial lagers emerged in the 20th century for people who prefer simple, cheap beers to tastier ones. Many but not all have become high in malt substitutes, low on hops, mashed and boiled fast, and fermented swiftly with little conditioning. The inevitable flavour flaws caused by these shortcuts are mostly hidden by serving them cold. To appreciate just how bad some of these beers are, drink them at room temperature.

In contrast, authentic German lagers ensure better ingredients by sticking to 100% malt and hops, while the Czechs prefer to squeeze every last gram of graininess from the malt by using decoction mashing. In both cases the hop recipes are paired carefully.

German blond lagers include **Helles**, a light, bright, highly attenuated quencher, originating from Munich, fuller, crisper **German Pils** from further north, and golden-blond **Märzen** (also Oktoberfestbier), which is fuller still, though Austrian versions are leaner. The main Czech or Bohemian lagers are fulsome, smooth and grainy **Světlý Ležák** (pronounced svet-ley lesh-ack) and the lighter, more quenching **Světlé Výčepní** (svet-ley vi-chep-ny).

Until the late 19th century most lagers were dark. In Germany brown **Dunkel** (sometimes **Munchener**) is near universal, while jet-black **Schwarzbier** is associated with the east. In general, both brown and black lagers are reviving, as with Czech **Tmavý** or **Černý**. Few amber lagers survived industrialisation, though recent years have seen the re-emergence of the original **Wiener** (or Vienna lager) from Austria, and of **Polotmavý** in the Czech Republic.

A couple of German variants worth getting to know are smoked **Rauchbier**

from Bamberg, and the original cold-stored (or 'lagered') beer, **Kellerbier**, from the surrounding region of Oberfranken.

Most authentic lagers are session beers, though a few are stronger. German Bock beers come as autumnal **Dunkles Bock**, springtime's **Maibock** (or Helles Bock) and Bavarian **Doppelbock**. Heavyweight experimental **Eisbock** also appears. Historically, Polish **Baltic Porter** should be a lager.

SESSION STRENGTH ALES

The concept of a 'session strength' beer is even more helpful when trying to understand ales and stouts. Indeed, EBCU's *Beer Styles of Europe and Beyond* uses the term to differentiate regular ales from those of 'sampling strength' and 'sipping strength'.

In classic UK session-strength **Cask Ale**, it is the 'cask' part of the description that is as important stylistically as the many sub-styles covered loosely by terms such as Mild,

CRAFT CORNER, LUXEMBOURG

Bitter, Best Bitter, and latterly Amber, Golden and so on.

The UK's greater contribution to beer development in recent decades has been through its historic styles, often more widely recreated abroad than at home. Older styles that have regained a footing in the UK include lactose-sweet **Milk Stout**, drier **Oatmeal Stout**, and a lighter type of brown stout increasingly termed **English Porter**. Malt-driven styles reviving slowly north of the border are known increasingly as **Scottish Heavy** (locally 80 shilling; 80/-) and **Scottish Export** (sometimes 90 shilling; 90/-).

Brewery records show no consistent differences between beers named 'Porter' or 'Stout' since around 1800. However, the way these beers were brewed in Ireland diversified from the British method around 1820, for the use of black malt ahead of brown, splitting further after 1880, when the use of roasted barley was licensed, making **Irish Stout** much drier.

In Germany, light amber **Altbier** from Düsseldorf and blond **Kölsch** from Cologne each undergo brief cold-conditioning but are ales by fermentation. Elsewhere in Europe, traditionally session strength ales were uncommon, though soft, pale Belgian **Spéciale** (or Speciaal) had its fans, as does regular French **Bière Brune**, with its distinctive rich, caramel streak.

SAMPLING STRENGTH ALES

For the last half-century the masters of stronger ales have been the Belgians, whose **Dubbel** is a mirror image of the old British **Double Brown** style, which is starting to re-appear. The Belgian type belies its strength through local brewing techniques that make drinkability, or 'balance' as its brewers prefer, the top priority.

Balance is achieved in different ways in **Saison**, whereby a cluster of earthy yeast strains work on clever hop recipes to create rustic flavours, and **Flemish Old Brown**, in which lactic acidity from ageing is offset by caramel flavours

BREWING TRADITIONS AND BEER STYLES

conjured from roasted malts.

The mostly Irish **Extra Stout**, while not so dry as its lighter form, should show a slightly aged edge from early mixed fermentation. In contrast, a French **Bière de Garde**, whether blonde, ambrée or brune, should retain big malt flavours despite extended keeping and be neither musty nor sharp.

SIPPING STRENGTH ALES

The expertise behind the strongest ales and stouts came from Victorian Britain and 20th century Belgium, the latter gifting us **Strong Golden**, the prosaic name given to pale, well-attenuated ales like Duvel, the rich, sweet, slightly honeyed power of **Tripel**, and the extremes of complexity found in **Dark Strong** (now sometimes Quadrupel), the latter two associated with the Trappist tradition of monastic brewing.

The surviving British forms include: **Scotch Ale** (or Wee Heavy), a full-on malt brew making slow but steady advances over the last five decades; a version of **Barley Wine** that features earthy, floral or marmalade notes, made entirely from pale malts but darkened with age, some with a vinous quality; sweet, roasted **Strong Export Stout**

(sometimes Tropical), full of caramel and alcohol; and **Imperial Stout**, an all-guns-blazing beer that challenges its brewer to attain drinkability at the extremes.

BEERS FROM OTHER GRAINS

In addition to those beers based entirely on malted barley, Europe has a long history of making beers from wheat and other grains. Best known are those from southern Germany, where cloudy, light-coloured **Hefeweizen**, brown, hazy **Dunkelweizen** and today's many variants from non-alcoholic and low alcohol, via clear **Kristallweizen** to hefty **Weizenbock** all feature, in varying degrees, banana, clove and nutmeg notes coming from specialist strains of yeast.

Belgian wheat beer, known as **Wit** (also Blanche or White) gains its spicy edge from dried citrus peel, coriander and other spices added to the boil. Variations from elsewhere include the light, smoked **Grodziskie** and strong, wheat-heavy **Schoeps** from Poland, plus light, lactic sour **Berliner Weiße**, sharp, lightly spiced **Gose** and sour, smoky **Lichtenhainer** from Germany.

Many small, independent French

breweries use spelt and buckwheat to create a growing range of specialist beers, just as in Estonia their peers are experimenting with using traditional brown rye in beers of many styles.

WILD AND FOLK BEERS

Other beer styles are more esoteric, some surviving for centuries, while others come from the imagination of newer brewers. Perhaps the most legendary is the Lambic family of beers – aged wheat beers, fermented by wild yeast, made at a dozen breweries in Brussels and neighbouring Payottenland. In their authentic or Oude (also Vieille) forms, these are found as draught **Lambic**, which when refermented with sugar becomes **Faro**, or if blended and bottled morphs into **Gueuze** (or Geuze). Steeping cherries or raspberries in Lambic creates, respectively, **Kriek** or **Framboise**.

The best-known folk beer in northern Europe is strong, sweet, rye-based **Sahti** from Finland, though Scandinavia and the Baltic rim have many other 'farmhouse' styles, featuring fermentation by a '**kveik**' yeast culture.

The beers emanating from southern Europe are altogether newer, often featuring the clever use of unusual ingredients, Italian brewers being the supreme architects. The best regarded thus far is cheekily named **IGA** (or Italian Grape Ale), which covers a group of funky styles that include grapes, grape must, or sometimes young wine.

THE CRAFT BEER DIMENSION

So much for the massive variety of heritage beer styles emanating from Europe. But what of the US-influenced beer styles most associated with the global rise of 'craft' beer?

In the beginning there was **IPA**, a phenomenon that began in the US in the 1990s. Although taking its initials from the old British style India Pale Ale, this new form was always about showing off the qualities of hops, in different combinations of bitterness, aroma and flavour.

Alternative forms have since evolved, at alcoholic strengths from zero to over 10% ABV, in every colour on beer's spectrum, from white to black, and more recently with degrees of haze running from misty to milky. If this continues, 'IPA' may yet become as meaningless a term as the word 'lager' became in the 1970s.

As well as experimenting with the limits of hops and haziness, many 'craft' brewers are playing with making sour beers, by use of controlled enzymatic activity, or **wild beers** from the introduction of slow yeast cultures. Adding fruit and other flavourings, usually in the form of syrups, essences and extracts is also now commonplace.

Only time will tell whether these creations last the distance, though having tasted hundreds of examples, my own feeling is that those with a lasting appeal are far outnumbered by the one-dimensional, sickly sweet and, when laced with vinegar or stomach acids, just plain unpleasant.

The more lasting contributions of the current wave of creative craft brewing to the future of beer will likely come from well-judged and practised fusions of craft era innovations with well-honed traditional techniques.

HOW TO DRINK BEER

Asking someone who has just bought a beer book to think about how they drink a beer may sound ridiculous, but stick with me and the question may start to make sense.

Let's begin with a basic equation:

Taste + Aroma = Flavour

The twin senses of smell and taste are intimately linked in the human brain, so the aroma from a beer can contribute up to a third of its flavours. This explains why the hop recipe is so important. Yet how often do you see someone swig beer direct from a bottle or can? Are they trying to reduce its flavour? Maybe.

Then turn your thoughts to temperature. Any beer that contains live yeast – be it a cask ale, a sedimented bottled ale or simply one that has not been pasteurised or microfiltered – will condition best and develop most flavour at between 9 and 13 degrees centigrade (°C). Yet how often is beer stored in a fridge or refrigerated cellar? Is the aim to restrict the beer? Probably not.

The same applies to the serving temperature. Beer flavours are optimal at around 12-15°C and yet bar owners and customers have become used to 'cold beer' at 4-8°C. As mentioned previously, in many industrial lagers, cheap recipes and rapid production methods can create noxious flavour components and one way to hide these is to chill the beer. Better beers should not be served ice cold. It is as simple as that.

Finally, spare a thought for presentation. The primped and waistcoated server pours half of your sedimented bottled ale into a glass, leaving its lees to well up in the remaining half, tainting its flavour. Was that really what they were trained to do? Indeed, were they trained at all?

The recent fashion for deliberately clouding up draught beers without giving thought to how the type of haze affects the beer's nature and flavour is just the latest in a long line of fashions designed to persuade beer lovers to drink with their eyes rather than their palates.

As with everything, drinking beer requires lifelong learning.

KNOW THE LOCALITY

For each of the destinations featured in this book I have made some pretty serious recommendations of where to drink, but don't let that stop you exploring.

In most parts of the world today, the nature of beer divides unevenly into two. By far the larger half is made up of commodity beers, where a relatively small number of familiar brands are traded at prices that appear low and yet hide some impressively high profit margins – make it cheap, price it high.

The smaller half is beers brewed for flavour, built on a wealth of local heritage and traditional beer styles, some going back centuries, coupled with ones from the more recent concept of craft brewing, which is really the research and development wing of the same trade. The economic model in this case has the beer costing whatever it does to make, with the aim of trying to sell it at an affordable price.

In Europe, many historically different beer cultures never quite died

BEERLOVERS, VIENNA

out and to this day have a lingering influence. For the modern beer drinker therefore, the most sensible use of any travel opportunity is to seek out those locally made beers that are either most associated with the city or region, or else come from the best local brewers.

Deciding what to drink
Determining which beers to drink depends to some extent on whether you are seeking ticks or understanding. (Those wanting to sample as many beers as possible so as to claim to have drunk more brands than 99.74% of the world's population can skip to the next bit.)

In the UK you should drink cask ales, plus some of the efforts to revive older beer styles; in Ireland try as many Stouts and Porters as you can find; in Scandinavia sip higher strength bottled ales; around the Baltic rim try to find a few rustic farmhouse beers; in Poland drink anything smoked or black; in the Czech Republic and Bavaria drink draught lagers; anywhere in Germany bag the variations on wheat beer, plus local specialities like Alt (in Düsseldorf), Kölsch (Cologne), Rauchbier (Bamberg) and Kellerbier (Oberfranken); in Italy drink beers with stuff added; and in France find Bière de Garde and ales made with spelt or buckwheat.

Drink bottled Belgian ales wherever and whenever you can, and wherever you are in Europe see how they are interpreting Pale Ales and IPA, Stout and Porter, strong Brown Ales and anything that is hop forward.

KNOWING YOUR BAR

In Europe the amount of beer sold for take-home is typically twice that sold in bars. The way a nation drinks is determined mostly by how its beers are taxed.

That said, thanks to the relative prosperity of Europe in the last three decades and the removal of physical and cultural borders, barriers and, in some cases, walls, ideas have inevitably spread through different cultures. A type of drinking institution associated with just one or two countries is now mimicked successfully in others, often with a local twist, while the originals absorb foreign habits. Think coffee machines in British pubs and vertical drinking in Belgian cafés.

New drinking spaces

Across much of Europe six essentially different types of beer venue are growing in number: on-site taprooms at breweries; simple brewery-owned taphouses in the local town; small, independent specialist beer bars; beer shops with tasting rooms; up-scale premises where a clever beer offer is part of a bigger all-round experience; and pre-COVID at least, lavish brewpubs with large food operations. A seventh category, places with a personal stamp that limit what they do to what they do well, also remain predictably popular.

In contrast, run-of-the-mill bars that smell of the street, whose staff are on zero hours contracts and the minimum wage, selling mostly brand name drinks and reheated food, fitted with identical cheap furnishings and too much advertising are tending to do badly. This too seems inevitable.

How to find a good pub

My personal working definition of a pub is that it is somewhere I can walk into and buy a beer, without needing to be a member, stay over or have to have a meal. By that definition, every country in Europe has pubs.

The skill is to carve a local variant by applying design features that reflect the local culture, which in turn is, of course, shaped in part by the type of drinking venues it prefers. This is a roundabout way of saying that not only does everywhere in Europe have pubs of sorts, the best of these speak to their nation's values and soul.

KNOWING YOUR BEER

My guess, from half a century of people watching, is that perhaps one-third of us care about the flavour, character and quality of what we consume. This may

LABIETUS, RIGA

be rising slowly as we re-acquaint ourselves with how food and drink are made, but even so, oppression by familiarity holds us back. We won't try it because we don't know it.

Best not to overthink this, perhaps. Choosing a beer is difficult enough without having to wonder what your choice says about who you are and how you think.

Which brands are best?

Few beer drinkers consider branding, yet large beer producers think about little else. Most beers found in supermarkets are the result of hundreds of careful decisions made about target demographics, imaging, market positioning, and the key concepts or people with which to associate the name of the beer.

For more on this subject, read Pete Brown's excellent *Beer by Design*, published by CAMRA Books in 2020-21.

In case you think this doesn't matter, in 2019 Brand Finance, one of the world's leading independent brand valuation companies, formally valued the Budweiser brand at US$ 7.52 billion, Bud Light at US$ 6.98 billion, Heineken at US$ 6.77 billion, and tenth-place Guinness at US$ 2.88 billion, headlining that a 'craft' brand had entered the global top 25 for the first time. BrewDog, in 19th position, was valued at US$ 1.5 billion.[1]

When it comes to choosing a traditional, heritage, craft or special beer from a lengthy beer menu, the branding considerations are rather different. What matters most are the beer style and, in the best cases, the brewery of origin.

[1] Beers 25 2019: The annual report on the most valuable and strongest beer brands, Brand Finance

CHOOSING A GOOD BEER

In a world with nigh on 30,000 breweries and 500,000 beers in circulation, develop whatever rules work for you. Here are mine:

- I avoid beers that have no stated brewery of origin on the label
- I trust a brewery more if it includes its name in its branding
- Beers that have funny or convoluted names rarely deliver
- Breweries that concentrate on a small core range of beers will get there
- A brewery that makes lots of flavoured beers is lost in the wilderness

WHAT TO EAT WITH YOUR BEER

It has become a badge of honour among beer writers to be able to recommend the type of brew to accompany particular foods. Having been around the scene longer than most, I should have risen to the challenge but held back because, in part, there are other beer writers who have more authority on the subject.

I also have a separate reservation. Having watched beer lovers at table over the years I reckon that a majority, or at least a substantial minority, are as careful in choosing what they eat as they are when picking a beer. However, as they approach beer number five, even those with impressively refined palates seem able to rationalise chucking a full plate of high-calorie filth down their necks.

So, for them and for you, consider this. Whenever studies are conducted to compare the body weight of people who drink beer with those who prefer wine, the former always weigh more. However, when the reasons for this are probed, the greater weight comes not from the beverage or its alcohol content, but from the accompanying diet. Wine drinkers are slimmer than beer drinkers because they eat better.

This may sound unfair, beveragist even, but as a child of the pie-and-a-pint era, not unfamiliar when younger with the after-pub curry, I can see that my own undisciplined eating over the decades has contributed to my own regrettable girth. When men like me overfeed, we add adipose tissue – or fat – to our abdomen, while women tend to add it more to their arms, thighs and bums.[2]

As an early adopter of craft beer drinking, I had hoped that this modern approach might come with learning more considered eating habits too. But no. The culinary bulwarks of the craft scene have become burgers, pizza, pasta and things like pulled pork, which as high-calorie companions to fermented carbs are no better than the older stuff. They just feel better, a triumph of image over content.

On the principle of do as I say rather than as I do, I would commend all long-distance beer travellers to consider the so-called Mediterranean diet, the original version of which came from Spain and included in it a couple of glasses of wine or beer each day. Its key ingredients are unrefined foods in the form of vegetables, nuts and fruit, supplemented by restrained amounts of meat, fish and cheese, not subject to elaborate processing and free from high-calorie sauces or sides of fried carbs.

This a great theory to bear in mind as you wade through the pages of recommendations I make for various must-try types of tasty local sludge, which by their nature are likely to be salted, to make you drink more, sugared to keep you alert, and fatted to fool your stomach into thinking it can take more beer. The hospitality trade is not stupid.

[2] Q&A: The truth about that beer belly (https://health.clevelandclinic.org/qa-the-truth-about-that-beer-belly/)

PICKING BEERS TO PAIR WITH YOUR FOOD

The principles of pairing beer with food are fairly simple. As a general rule, lighter beers pair better with delicately flavoured dishes and heavier beers with grandmother cooking. That said, it tends to take a heftier beer to withstand the assault of a highly spiced dish, while lighter, hoppier beers can often counter the tendency of fattier dishes to clog up the palate.

Salty snacks can diminish a malt-driven beer, with more hop-forward beers tolerating them better, though clashing badly with anything pickled or in other ways acidic.

If you have ordered something blackened by searing, choose a beer with some hop bite to it, or if a creamy sauce is likely to dominate, try softening it down with a wheat beer.

A simple rule that is worth transporting from bar life to home life is that beer tends to pair far better with cheeses than wine does, the sharper edges of the latter clanging with similar properties found in many better cheeses. If you don't believe me, try out a few recommendations that I am proud

not only to have stolen from, but also experienced at the hand of, my good friend and colleague Stephen Beaumont.

With a hard cheese like cheddar, manchego or even pecorino try taking a

UK-style Pale Ale of some calibre; with young gouda, or one of the lesser-known rubbery cheeses found in northern Europe, try a Bock; deploy a big, malty Barley Wine or malt-driven strong Brown Ale to go with a serious blue cheese like stilton or gorgonzola; or a roasty Porter or Stout with a soft French cheese like camembert or brie.

Less well-appreciated perhaps is the superiority of many types of beer over wine when accompanying a pudding or dessert, the rule in most cases being that the beer should at least match its sweetness. The common exception is when pairing with chocolate, where more important is roastiness, or the dark flavours of liquorice or stewed fruit.

For me, however, the greatest pleasure comes from finding that random pairing that happens to work for no obvious reason, such as the great Flemish pairing of hand-rolled shrimp croquettes, fried fresh parsley and Rodenbach Grand Cru – a gift to the world from the astute palate of another of my collaborators, American beer writer Joe Stange.

TRADITIONAL BAR FOODS

So much for the theory. Now for the practice.

Rarely do food-selling bars, cafés and pubs, or even those rare beasts, restaurants with substantial beer menus, routinely construct their offers with pairings in mind.

The menu at one of the pubs I have been pleased to call my local at some point in my life invariably included 'Prawn Cocktail, because this is a pub!'. This was a nod to the fact that pub chefs often fall victim to a desire to put an item on a menu because 'people like it', regardless of whether it has any place alongside beer, or indeed anywhere else. A nation's best-known dishes all too often exist because they were once recommended by a TV chef from an era that is otherwise long gone.

And yet if these things weren't there, we would surely miss them.

In Belgium I like to see a vispannetje (pieces of fish cooked in a cheese sauce on a skillet) on the menu, or a waterzooi (chicken or goose braised in a cream sauce); in the Czech Republic I need my gulaš (black meat drowned in dark gravy) or svíčková (beef drowned in not-so-dark gravy), with dumplings; and in Germany I must have pork cooked in one of three ways but prepared in many hundreds.

Face it, what really shapes the menus that appear in beer venues is not the suitability of the dish to a place where beer is king, but whether or not it seems to suit the sort of place the owners think that their customers think it is.

So, my advice as you plan your culinary adventure for the coming evening, or if you are so inclined, the whole trip, is to work out what the locality you are visiting is famed for producing, then remember what I said at the beginning about beer drinkers being overfed, and refrain from ordering them. Instead, concentrate on finding the one healthy option on a menu so absurdly long that all it really tells you is that half the stuff comes via the microwave from the deep freeze, and eat humbly.

Or not, as the mood takes you.

TASTY MORSELS

Leaving fancy cooking behind us, let us turn instead to the side-plate.

If I could command the world's beer venues to adopt one habit, it would be to resurrect the tradition of serving beers with a nibble. Not the chemically

enhanced crisp or salt-blasted fried nut of Sunday lunch at a posher boozer, but the edible thank you gifted by a grateful patron to one who orders a decent beer, or the small portion of something bought to delay the need to dine.

In the Netherlands, owners of small 'brown' bars serve monkey nuts in their shells, so that customers will discard these and tread them into the floor to keep it oiled; or hard-boiled eggs, protected by their shells from the smoky atmosphere, back in the day.

Mediterranean bars offer pistachios or olives, while their Belgian equivalents serve small cubes of rubbery cheese with celery salt and tangy mustard. Spreading a pungent sheep's cheese on dry bread and serving it with radish lets you know you are in Brussels' market garden, Payottenland.

Or nibble on bits of pig. Slices of salami or saucisson sec appear on bar tops in many parts of Europe, sometimes supplanted in Spain by small nicks cut from a joint of iberico or serrano ham, depending on its breed. For beef, in Italy take dry-cured bresaola, or in Amsterdam, lightly spiced and smoked, lean, minced ossenworst. In Brussels, swap to the green-speckled chicken brawn, kip-kap.

Hot meats are indulgent, like tiny, salt-soaked pork souvlaki in Athens, or Italian polpetti meatballs, distinguished from scrumptious Dutch bitterballen for the absence of volcanic heat, undiagnosable goo and luminescent mustard.

The Baltic states offer pan-fried rye bread rubbed in garlic, while heading south the breads get bigger: salted Bavarian Pretzel (which bears no relation to the packet snack); the crescent-shaped kifli, or bite-sized savoury pogácsa in Hungary; or Spain's small, filled pastry pockets, empanadas.

Pa amb tomàquet, the tomato-spread, stale bread slices of Barcelona, may be a distant cousin of Italian crostini, yet share traits with patatas bravas, spicy tomato-topped potato cubes, though these are a world apart from placki ziemniaczane potato pancakes in Poland.

It is all part of the show and makes me wonder whether four pork scratchings, laid out neatly on a paper napkin, should be the classic companion to a special pint of cask?

THE EUROPEAN BEER EVENTS CALENDAR

Beer festivals, and other events designed to celebrate beer, vary in their origins, purposes, traditions and aplomb. While most festivals can claim to be promoting beer, some do this by showcasing the diversity of a local beer culture, dispensing small measures to encourage visitors to taste a wide array, others do so by concentrating on volume in order to make money. The best attract volunteer help, while the worst use plastic glasses.

COVID caused most beer festivals in Europe to be suspended, in some cases leading to their demise, while others have changed their dates. As organisers try to recoup their losses for two dry years, it is more important than ever to check their current status before planning any trip around attendance, and to book ahead whenever possible, if only to avoid entrance queues.

What follows is my highly personal pick of the events in Europe for which I would most like a free ticket.

JANUARY

BRAUKUNST LIVE!

(braukunst-live-muenchen.de) is usually held in Munich in late January or early February as part of an industry gathering that brings together under one roof all the German craft and heritage brewers who mean business. This is one for beer tasting and networking, with not a litre-sized Maß in sight.

FEBRUARY

BEER & FOOD ATTRACTION

(beerandfoodattraction.it) is another trade event that opens to the public, at the Fiera in Rimini (Italy) in the second half of February. Hidden within a huge trade fair that is held in the sort of exhibition centre that gets its own train station, it hosts the country's best collection of booths run by mostly Italian brewers.

APRIL

ZYTHOS BIERFESTIVAL

(zbf.be), held at the Brabanthal exhibition centre on the outskirts of Leuven on the final weekend in April, is consumer-hosted and exhibitor-run. It is open to any brewer in Belgium to attend, on a first-come-first-served basis. Brewers are more likely to be there early in the day. There is a regular bespoke bus from the train station.

MAY

BREW//LDN

(brewldn.com), formerly Craft Beer Rising, was rebranded to lose the C-word, but stayed in London and for 2022 has shifted to early May. The largest and classiest of the UK events promoting CFT//BR and CFT//BWRS and their carb-peddling fellow travellers. The music is intrusive but there are great conversations.

🔴 VIENNA CRAFT BIER FEST

(craftbierfest.at) in the capital's Marx Halle used to happen on a Friday and Saturday in November. Since moving to its mid-May date in 2020 it has not actually happened. It is really rather a sedate appreciation of the Austrian beer scene, from the smallest to the largest, and all the more enjoyable for that.

🔴 THE ØLFESTIVAL

(ølfestival.dk) in Copenhagen is organised by the hugely successful Danske Ølentusiaster consumer group (ale.dk), with up to 100 Danish and foreign breweries running stalls, plus some more public-facing suppliers. Back to its regular spot in the second half of May, it is quite simply one of the best run festivals in Europe.

🔵 RICHEMENT BIÈRE

(richement-biere.fr) has run since 1998 at Richement, near Metz (France), alongside a small trade show. It draws around 40 breweries mostly from France, with a few from neighbouring parts of French-speaking Europe. Usually held in January, COVID shifted it to the last weekend in May. Includes guest lectures in French.

JUNE

🔴 WROCŁAWSKI FESTIWAL DOBREGO PIWA

(festiwaldobregopiwa.pl), held at the stadium in Wrocław throughout the first weekend of June is the largest in Poland and deliberately framed to be quite educational. Run by a cultural events company in the city and aimed at both beer lovers and the general public but serving up well over 1,000 beers.

TALLINN CRAFT BEER WEEKEND

(tcbw.ee & FB/tallinncraftbeer) in mid-June has a huge regional following and usually sells out in advance. However, with so much good beer in the city if you don't get a ticket enjoy the bars being a little quieter. Parallel events include the Tallinn Crap Beer event, showcasing the worst in modern brewing.

🔴 FRÄNKISCHES BIERFEST

(bierfest-franken.de) in Nuremberg (Germany) runs for five days in late

TEH EUROPEAN BEER EVENTS CALENDAR

June or 800m each side, depending on how you measure it. Around 40 mostly Franconian breweries sell beers from stalls that line either side of a meandering route through the old Imperial Castle grounds. Great atmosphere.

JULY

 SUURET OLUET

(suuretoluet.fi) is a touring beer event that runs through six Finnish cities between May and October. The largest gathering has now expanded to take up Tuesday to Saturday on each of the last two weeks of July, just behind Helsinki station, featuring mostly Finnish ale and Sahti brewers, with a few Estonian guests.

ALLADOOCH ANNAFEST

(alladooch-annafest.de) in Forchheim (Germany) takes up eleven days astride St Anna's day (26 July), during which time the 23 Upper Franconian breweries that operate Bierkeller or Biergarten venues on the Kellerwald hillside work them all flat out, alongside many musical events, in this good-natured Bavarian festival.

AUGUST

 THE GREAT BRITISH BEER FESTIVAL

(gbbf.org.uk), held in London in early August, is the largest event in the beer world to be organised and staffed by consumers. This huge celebration of UK and imported cask ale, plus much more besides, is unquestionably the continent's finest beer event.

SEPTEMBER

VILLAGGIO DELLA BIRRA

(villaggiodellabirra.com) held near Buonconvento (Italy) in the first week of September, is the only event included here that has yet to commit to running again. Delightfully impossible and much-loved, this elite gathering of small brewers draws thousands to a remote farm in Tuscany.

OCTOBER

 SALON DU BRASSEUR

(salondubrasseur.com) in Nancy (France) is a trade event run by independent brewers, held over a weekend in October, also aimed at the public. It attracts some of the best brewers from France and promotes the massive rise in craft brewing that has

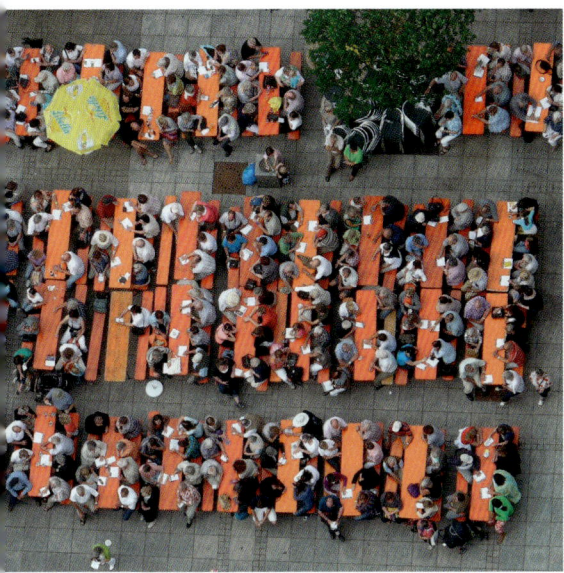

led to France having the most breweries of any country in Europe.

DECEMBER

🇸🇪 STOCKHOLM BEER AND WHISKY FESTIVAL

(stockholmbeer.se) shifted in 2021 from two weekends in September and October to just one at the start of December. Pretty expensive, seriously impressive and cleverly constructed, it celebrates all types of beer in Sweden and beyond, adding a whisky chaser. Gives good advice on how to taste.

🇪🇸 BARCELONA BEER FESTIVAL

(barcelonabeerfestival.com) ditched its regular March slot for December in 2021 but kept up its reputation as one of most vibrant and important beer festivals anywhere, attracting the greatest annual gathering of craft brewers in southern Europe, thanks to a parallel trade event. Also features Latin American street food.

🇧🇪 KERSTBIER FESTIVAL

(kerstbierfestival.be), on the third weekend of December in the north Belgian town of Essen, tries to serve up every Belgian winter beer on the market. Held in a sparsely converted sports hall, at the furthest end from its station of a remote town with no accommodation. So, of course, it usually sells out well in advance.

THE GROUND RULES

The key to enjoying a beer festival, I find, is not to expect too much. Expect the building to be cold and draughty early on and unpleasantly hot later; the beer to be plentiful but below its best; the food limited to deep-fried carbs and sugar-enhanced dough balls; the music to be loud and inappropriate; and the crowd to look just as bewildered as you feel. That way the actual experience can be a lot better than expected, or at least a relief.

The only must-do is to plan your transport arrangements down to the last detail, including having no qualms whatever about casting your friends adrift if they don't make the rendezvous on time.

The beer matters little. It is the conversations and meeting of minds with complete strangers from far distant parts that you will take home with you, and which will draw you to repeat the experience, some day.

TEH EUROPEAN BEER EVENTS CALENDAR

THE PRICE OF BEER IN EUROPE

North is expensive, east is cheap, the rest is pretty average, and that's it. Almost, though there is a bit more to it than that.

By far the largest contributing factor to the price of a beer is the extent to which it is taxed – directly or indirectly. This in turn depends on national government policies that often reflect how early 20th-century law-makers saw the relative importance and dangers of beer brewing and of alcohol more generally. While this varies a lot from country to country, no European nation takes more tax from beer than Britain.

Since 2011 the total amount of excise duty raised annually from beer in the UK has wavered between €3.9 and €4.4 billion. No other European country has yet raised as much as €1 billion in any one year. What is more, excise duty is included in the baseline price of the beer, which means it is subject to percentage-based mark-ups all along its supply chain, with VAT at 20% added to all at the point of sale.

Britain is not entirely alone in placing a high toll on beer drinkers. Three of Europe's smaller nations, Finland, Norway and Ireland, take even more per glass. However, even if Russia, Ukraine and Belarus were added to the table opposite of Europe's more populous nations, the UK's place as top tax-raiser remains.

Taxing beer heavily creates a number of problems. Socially, it drives people with a degree of alcohol dependency to cheaper forms of alcohol, or to other drugs, giving up food or whatever else is required in order to afford it. Economically, brewing industries beset by high taxes in their home markets tend to produce smaller amounts for export, while having to thin out their products for domestic consumption.

OTHER TAXES AND SUBSIDIES

Regular travellers will know that the price charged for beer in bars varies significantly, not always in line with relative excise duty. This is often because other tax regimes are applied, some quite subtly. For example, in France exceptionally high overheads apply to some types of licenced premises, while in Belgium a 100% mark-up is tolerated in cafés, in part because the three separate licenses required to operate them – one for the premises, one for the management, one for the owner – carry inevitable on-costs.

Meanwhile more subtle effects are in play. The virtual absence of collaboration between national farming industries in Europe in the post-War period led in 1962 to the first Common Agricultural Policy (CAP). As part of this, vineyards and winemakers benefitted from subsidies for being part of the agricultural community, while maltsters and brewers were considered to be in manufacturing, so did not. Depending on how it is measured, the CAP subsidy to wine drinkers is thus far between €15 and €40 billion.

That said, many countries support smaller independent breweries by exempting them from some excise duty. This makes sound political sense because it is here, and in the businesses that sell their products, that most of the new jobs in the beer trade are created.

LIGHTER BEER ALLOWANCES

The other common government subsidy, of sorts, is the excise reductions allowed for low-alcohol beers. While the logic of these appears obvious, this does not necessarily lead to lower prices, as the techniques of building distinctive flavour into a low- or no-alcohol beer are complex and often more expensive than in regular brewing.

THE TAX RAISED FROM BEER THROUGH EXCISE DUTY AND VAT ACROSS EUROPE IN 2019

COUNTRY	Population (in millions)	Excise in €millions[4]	Excise in € per head	Beer per head a year (litres)	Excise Duty € per litre	Duty on 33cl of 5% ABV[3]	VAT in 2019
Germany	83.1	617	7.42	100	0.07	0.03	19%
UK	66.9	4156	62.1	71	0.87	0.35	20%
France	67.3	987	14.7	33	0.45	0.13	20%
Italy	59.7	713	11.9	35	0.34	0.12	22%
Spain	47.1	356.8	7.6	52	0.15	0.03	21%
Poland	38	786.7	20.7	98	0.21	0.08	23%
Romania	19.4	132.8	6.85	86	0.08	0.03	19%
Netherlands	17.3	422	24.4	71	0.34	0.13	21%
Belgium	11.5	201	17.5	68**	0.26	0.08	21%
Greece	10.7	198.1	18.5	37	0.5	0.21	24%
Czech Republic	10.7	184.8	17.3	142	0.12	0.05	21%
Portugal	10.3	93.9	9.2	53	0.17	0.07	23%
Sweden	10.3	411.8	40	58*	0.69	0.32	25%
Hungary	9.8	147.9	15.1	70	0.22	0.07	27%
Austria	8.9	189.7	21.3	107	0.2	0.08	20%
Switzerland	8.6	107.5	12.5	55	0.23	±0.08	7.70%
Bulgaria	7	40.3	5.8	74	0.08	0.03	20%
Denmark	5.8	110.1	19	62	0.31	0.11	25%
Finland	5.5	651.7	118.5	73	1.62	0.63	24%
Slovakia	5.5	59.5	10.8	75	0.14	0.06	20%
Norway	5.3	647.4*	122.2	51	2.4	±0.80	25%
Ireland	4.9	421	85.9	77	1.12	0.37	23%

* = 2018 data   ** = 2016 data

By EU law the minimum amount of excise that must be levied equates to just €0.03 on a 33cl bottle of 5% ABV beer.

Sources: [3] European Beer Trends 2020 edition, Brewers of Europe
[4] Elke Asen, Beer Taxes in Europe (taxfoundation.org/beer-taxes-in-europe-2021/)

ABOUT AMSTERDAM

Population: City 745,000; metropolitan area 1,165,000

Local breweries: 't IJ (Duvel Moortgat), Oedipus (Heineken), De Prael, Butcher's Tears, De 7 Deugden, Troost, Two Chefs, plus a dozen others.

Rail: The busy Amsterdam Centraal station, on the waterfront at the heart of the city, has direct connections with Antwerp (±16 a day; 1.1-1.6 hours); Brussels (±22 a day; 1.75-2.75 hours); Berlin (±6 a day; 6.2-6.5 hours); Paris (3 a day; 3.3-5.5 hours); and via Eurostar with London St Pancras (3 a day; 4 hours).

Airport: Amsterdam Schiphol airport is 20km southwest of the city centre and has direct connections with most UK airports. Up to a dozen trains an hour run to Centraal station at €4.70 each way. All other modes of transport are madness.

Currency: Euro (€)

AMSTERDAM

Ask any reasonably informed beer lover how ale is doing in the world and most can tell you that the Brits and Belgians make some pretty good ones and the Americans are going wild. The more switched on might mention Italy and Scandinavia. Few are likely to name the country that has been perhaps Europe's biggest success story this past decade – the Netherlands.

A dozen years ago Amsterdam was synonymous with cheaply made global brands like Heineken and Amstel. A connoisseur's beer trip to the city was reliant on specialist beer bars stocking good ranges of imports. Today, there are over 400 functioning Dutch breweries and another couple of hundred firms marketing small-run brews made by others. Expect Stouts, Porters, IPAs, Pale Ales, Barley Wines, wheat and rye beers, all the usual add-ons and dollops of attitude.

The people who make up the stag parties found weaving round Amsterdam's sex and drugs areas are getting older. Cool intoxication in this rapidly changing city is nowadays more about DIPA than dope. Shabby chic drinking spaces run by young entrepreneurs mimic strangely the heritage of old brown cafés – where centuries of nicotine staining pre-date the smoking ban.

If you are into great art collections the city's well-worn Van Gogh and Rijksmuseum are OK but find time for the Micro Art Amsterdam exhibition (microartamsterdam.com) ahead of these. Ignore the Heineken Experience and instead explore the wider beer culture.

BEER VENUES

The old Amsterdam beer scene relied on a few consistent performers standing high above the mass. The current scene is way broader but features experimentation, so expect some rough to come with the smooth. In addition to the locals, watch out for Dutch beers from Emelisse, Maximus, Uiltje, Kees, Ramses, Duits & Lauret, Bronckhorst, Eindhoven, Kompaan, Oersoep and many others, plus older hands Jopen and Trappist brewers La Trappe and Zundert.

▶ ARENDSNEST

 Herengracht 90 - arendnest.nl
Fr & Sa 12.00-02.00; others 12.00-24.00

Two canals west of Nieuwezijds Voorburgwal in the centre, this bucket list beer destination was, twenty years ago, no more than the optimistic hunch of a young Dutch beer campaigner intent on championing exclusively Dutch beers. It used to stock beer from every brewery, but when they topped 150 decided to concentrate on the most interesting. Around one-third are on draught. Hosts regular tastings. No food.

▶ IN DE WILDEMAN

📍 Kolksteeg 3 – indewildeman.nl
shut Su; Fr & Sa 12.00-02.00; others 12.00-01.00

Visiting this delightfully accomplished, memorable and music-free beer café, located between pedestrianised Nieuwendijk and Nieuwezijds Voorburgwal in the centre, remains a highlight of any year for me. Dedicated to beer in all its traditions and stocking no duds on a list of ±250, it has been in my global top ten beer destinations for decades. Set in an old distillery, its subtle modernisation over the years is seamless, so just sit back and absorb. Small snacks available.

▶ GOLLEM

🚪 Raamsteeg 4 – cafegollem.nl
Fr-Sa 12.00-02.00; Su 12.00-01.00; others 16.00-01.00

South of Dam Square, to the west before the first canal, this broadly unchanged, small and cosy brown café is where I first became acquainted with Belgian beer, 45 years ago. No food, no frills beyond a few candles; just a selection of ±200 beers. It may have been the first bar in the world to chalk its list on the walls. It screams hard-working authenticity.

▶ HOMELAND

🍴 🚪 Kattenburgerstraat 5 – brouwerijhomeland.nl
variable opening – bus 48: Kattenburgerstraat

Not the greatest beer bar in Amsterdam but the only set-up to run a taphouse, a restaurant, some letting rooms and a bunch of serviced apartments for longer stays, thus making it a unique resource. It's also on the waterfront, a 15-minute walk from 't IJ brewery taphouse at Funenkade 7. Thought you should know.

▶ FOEDERS

🚪 Ceintuurbaan 257 – foeders.amsterdam
Fr-Sa 14.00-03.00; others 14.00-01.00 – metro: Wibautstraat; or tram 4: Ceintuurbaan

This plain but smart specialist beer bar is not one you will find by accident. Aside from the 40 draught lines, the specialty here is 'wild' and 'sour' beers, with its Belgian owner pitching better Dutch craft examples alongside a heavy selection of proper Lambics and oak-aged ales from his homeland. Light snacks only.

FOEDERS

AMSTERDAM

▸ BIERKONING
🛈 Paleisstraat 125 – bierekoning.nl
Su 12.00-19.00; Mo 12.00-18.00; others 11.00-19.00

A block and a half west of Dam Square, at the least convenient stopping point for drivers in the whole of Amsterdam is one of the world's great beer shops. Staggering along since 1985 and still stocking around 1,500 beers, plus glasses and schwag, this is the place from which to take home the ones you missed.

▸ ELFDE GEBOD
🛈 Zeedijk 5 – gollem.nl
Fr-Su from 14.00; others from 16.00

The 'Eleventh Commandment' is a short walk from Centraal Station, a former Belgian bar that is now part of the same small chain as Gollem. No food, just 175 beers in an implausibly small and sometimes crowded café.

▸ MIKKELLER AT MOREBEER
🛈 Lange Leidsedwarsstraat 4 – mikkelleratmorebeer.nl – *daily from 16.00 – trams 2, 11, 12: Prinsengracht*

As Beer Loves Food, this deliberately understated beer and food bar was created by the guys who started Arendsnest (above). Now it's a sort of collab between them and Danish gypsy emperor Mikkeller. Rave reviews for both beer and food, though some will see it as a front for mostly hazy craft beer and a range of burgers, pulled meats and so on. Small and strangely backstreet in its ambience.

Other places to drink beer include brewery taphouses, such as **Walhalla** (Spijkerkade 10 – walhallacraftbeer.nl) and Heineken-spiked **Oedipus** (Gedempt Hamerkanaal 85 – oedipus.com), each walkable from the IJplein ferry behind Centraal station; **De Prael Oudezijds** (Oudezijds Armsteeg 26 – depraeloudezijds.nl) in the centre; and

OEDIPUS

BEER BREAKS

OEDIPUS

Butcher's Tears (Karperweg 45 – butchers-tears.com).

The Netherlands's other alcoholic creation is jenever, the original gin and good enough to be slurped neat at remarkable bars like **Wijnand Fockink** (Pijlsteeg 31 – Wynand-fockink.nl – daily 14.00-21.00), **Ooievaar** (Olofspoort 1 – proehlokaaldeooievaar.nl – daily from 12.00), or **'t Kelkje** (Oudezijds Achterburgwal 164 – kelkje.nl – shut Mo-Tu; Fr-Su 15.00-21.00; others 16.00-21.00), which pairs them with German and Czech lagers.

NEED TO KNOW

In normal times, Amsterdam is rammed year-round, especially at weekends, though Sunday nights are generally quieter and the unimaginative tend to stick to predictable places.

Accommodation: To stay in the centre, book well in advance. If nothing affordable is available in town, check around Sloterdijk station, halfway from the centre to Schiphol Airport. Make full use of any locked safe facility.

Getting around: The trams, buses and metro are all run by GVB. Trams go to most places, buses to the rest, while the metro is more for commuters and visiting suburbs. The easiest ticket is the OV-chipkaart, bought on arrival and also valid on trains. Use it to tap in and out of buses, trams or trains. GVB day tickets for 24, 48, 72, 96, 120 or 168 hours are also available but are harder to find. Single tickets no longer exist.

Food: Dutch cooking this century mirrors that of the UK, meaning the best has become world class, while cheaper options are either from the developing world or else health-challenging. As an exception take a raw, filleted herring each morning from a streetside stall. The top ethnic cuisine is Indonesian, best when from a Toko shop.

Hints: The city wakes up around 10.30. Tipping is included but rounding up the bill is appreciative. Don't walk in the cycle lane. Tim Skelton's superbly researched and written *Beer in the Netherlands 2* (Skelton Ink, 2020) is an essential companion.

ABOUT ANTWERP

- **Population:** City 460,000; metropolitan area 1,053,000
- **Local breweries:** De Koninck (Duvel Moortgat), Antwerpse Brouw Compagnie and others.
- **Rail:** The Majestic Antwerp Centraal station is at the heart of the New Town and on the high-speed train network. It has direct connections with Amsterdam (±16 a day; 1.1-1.6 hours); Brussels (±45 per day; 0.5-1 hour); and Paris (10+ per day; 2.1-3 hours).
- **Airport:** Antwerp airport flies mostly to holiday destinations with no direct UK connection.
- **Currency:** Euro (€)

ANTWERP

The cultural capital of Flanders is Belgium's largest port, a home to the diamond trade and a great repository of fine art. It was also a centre for the development of printing, so try to find time to visit the Plantin-Moretus Museum on Vrigdagmarkt.

Belgium was, along with the UK, West Germany and Czechoslovakia, one of the four countries to retain some vestige of a beer heritage into the final quarter of the 20th century and Antwerp was the crucible of the Belgian beer revival in the 1980s. Uniquely for that time, this spanned an exceptional variety of national styles, manifested mostly in bottle-conditioned examples.

Bizarrely for the context perhaps, the city's most iconic beer is the one often considered its plainest. De Koninck, served filtered but unpasteurised on draught, should be ordered by the bolleke (pronounced in the same way as bollocker). It is the epitome of an Antwerp-style malty Pale Ale, on a par with Düsseldorf's Altbier or Scotland's Heavy. To be fully appreciated it should be drunk with the blinkers removed.

BEER VENUES

For those who were discovering Belgian beer in the 1980s, the grey Gothic backstreets of Antwerp's Old Town were a grotto of hidden gems. Some of the beer bars of the early days remain, though now outnumbered by ones that complement the intentions of the old to a newer model. Thanks to complex licensing arrangements, no two bars are the same, in character, design or even purpose.

➤ ANTWERPSE BROUW COMPAGNIE TAPROOM

❶ ⓜ Indiestraat 21 – seef.be
daily from 12.00 – tram 24: Cadix

In an old warehouse district that served the harbours to the north of the centre, the huge taphouse of this small, independent 2017 start-up serves all their regular and experimental beers, backed up by a long menu of substantial and interesting bar snacks. It expanded rapidly and made good use of its huge courtyard during COVID.

➤ BEER LOVERS

❶ Rotterdamstraat 105 – beerloversbar.be
shut Tu; Fr-Su from 15.00; others from 16.00 – tram 12: Deconcinck

Dark but breezy craft beer bar, a short walk from Centraal station, in the New Town. They have respect for beers of all genres, so there are enough older and imported beers to keep everyone happy. Generally accepted as the best beer bar in the city currently. Rarely closed before midnight, much later at weekends. Nibbles only.

➤ DR BEER

❶ ❷ ⓜ Adriaan Brouwerstraat 31 – drbeer.be
shut Mo-Tu; others from 16.00 – tram 7: Antwerpen Brouwersvliet (northbound)

To the north of the Waasland tunnel, as the Old Town merges into the dockland area, this beer café was founded in 2019 to do everything right. In delightful surroundings the owners and staff talk beer with love and knowledge, giving guidance on flavours and matching their 100+ carefully chosen beers with excellent cheeses and cold cuts.

▶ BILLIE'S

🛈 🍴 Kammenstraat 12 – billiesbier.be

shut Tu; Sa-Su from 15.00; Mo from 18.00; others from 16.00 – many trams & buses: Groenplaats

In a side street off the Old Town's main square Groenplaats, this modern beer café and food bar is crammed into an old building that never thought it would be this popular. The ever-changing list of 150 beers is supplemented by good plates of Flemish-Craft fusion cuisine in the evenings. Can be rammed at weekends. Its related Bottle Shop (Aalmoezenierstraat 38 – We-Su) is good for take-home.

▶ ERNST

🛈 🍴 Ernest van Dijckkaai 20 – cafeernstantwerp.be

shut Mo-Tu; others 15.00-23.00, Fr-Sa 14.00) – many trams & buses: Groenplaats

On the road that parallels the Schelde, between Suikkerui and Vlasmarkt, is this chilled, chic craft beer and natural wines bar with a few cocktails and plates of food. Its hefty beer list blurs the line creatively between wine and beer, with modern sour and wild beers, a few Lambics, and some others distinctly non-binary, on an interesting list.

▶ KULMINATOR

🛈 Vleminckveld 32 – FB/kulminator.friends

shut Su-Mo; others 11.00-18.00 – tram 4, 12: Mechelseplein

Run by the same dedicated couple for nearly four decades. Nowadays a daytime café, its main attraction is a vast collection of vintage ales, mostly but not exclusively

Belgian, sourced over the decades. Much-loved and lived-in, it tends to shut over Easter, Christmas and early August, or whenever they fancy taking a well-earned break.

▶ OUD ARSENAAL

🛈 Maria Pijpelinckxstraat 4 – dorstvlegel.be
shut Mo-Tu; Sa-Su 07.30-19.30; others 10.00-22.00

A brilliant local boozer, up the way from the Rubenshuis museum in the artist's former home, has 90 years of authenticity behind it. Its hours are honed to local trade rather than the tourists in nearby hotels. Its single bar has enamel plaques, carved oak and floor tiling. There are 60 beers but no food, not even on the terrace.

NEED TO KNOW

The crowds head for the famous Cathedral and the Royal Museum of Fine Arts, but if that is not you, head down to the quay and take a boat tour round the almighty port. Beer-wise, central Antwerp withers on Mondays and Tuesdays. For the rest of the week be aware that one local specialty is weather, seasons sometimes changing every hour.

Accommodation: Aim to stay somewhere between Centraal station and the river. The chronic shortage of small or family-run hotels forces prices up much of the time. Apartments are better value but take care with the location and what the description excludes.

Getting around: Most of Antwerp is walkable. Its buses and trams are operated by De Lijn. Tickets are cheaper bought in advance at supermarkets or newsagents. Options include single tickets (€2.50); 10-trip passes (€16); 24 hours (€7.50); 72 hours (€15); or an Antwerp City Card enabling free admission to many attractions (72 hours = €48).

Food: Flemish food comes as grandmother style, local specialty, advanced wizardry, and steak or steamed mussels with frites (not fries). To visit and eat only fast food is a wasted opportunity. The Van Tricht cheese shop (41 Fruithoflaan) is among the best in the world.

Hints: Tips are included but round up for good service. Don't walk on the cycle lanes or tram lines. Don't even think of buying a diamond.

ATHENS

The Greek capital is peppered with the sort of antiquities that more general travel guides adore. What they won't tell you is that, inadvertently, Greece's financial crisis fanned the early flames of a local beer revolution.

At its simplest, young Greeks were starting to enjoy imported beers when their economy turned to hummus back in 2015. So, the earlier pioneers of Greek craft brewing decided to import the ingredients instead and learn to produce local imitations that were at least as good as the newly unaffordable imports; a plan that succeeded.

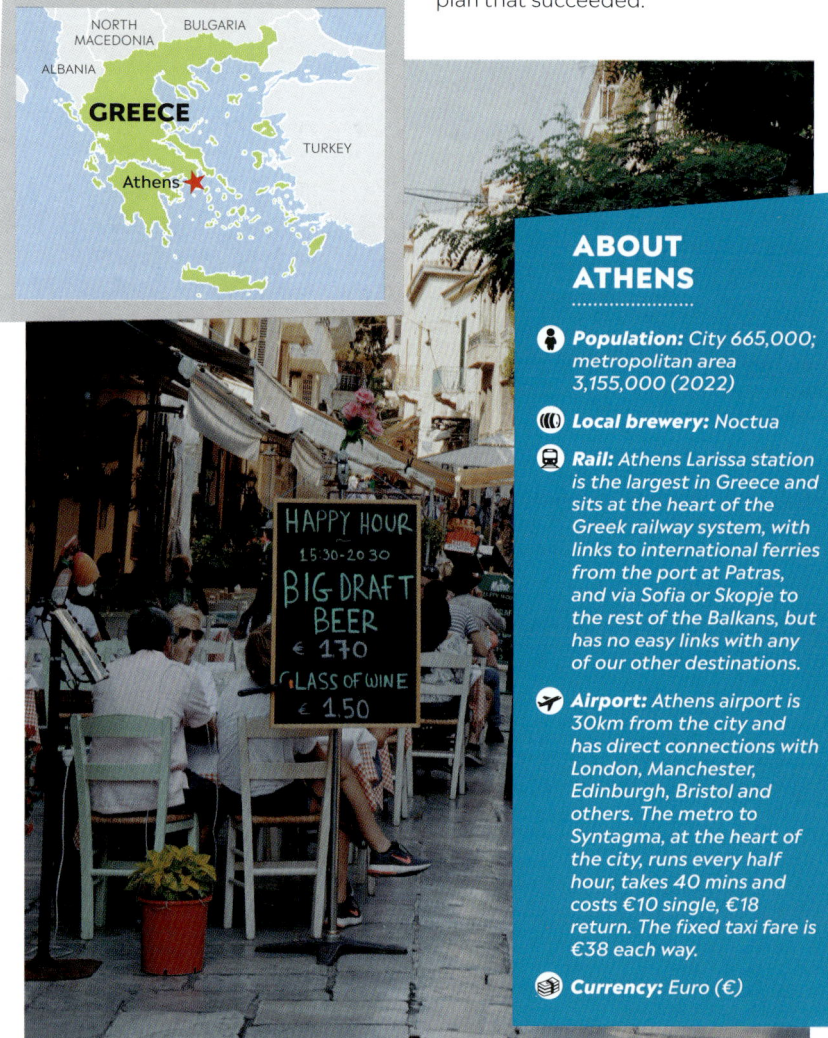

ABOUT ATHENS

- **Population:** City 665,000; metropolitan area 3,155,000 (2022)

- **Local brewery:** Noctua

- **Rail:** Athens Larissa station is the largest in Greece and sits at the heart of the Greek railway system, with links to international ferries from the port at Patras, and via Sofia or Skopje to the rest of the Balkans, but has no easy links with any of our other destinations.

- **Airport:** Athens airport is 30km from the city and has direct connections with London, Manchester, Edinburgh, Bristol and others. The metro to Syntagma, at the heart of the city, runs every half hour, takes 40 mins and costs €10 single, €18 return. The fixed taxi fare is €38 each way.

- **Currency:** Euro (€)

BEER VENUES

The mix of bar types in the city is as broad as the style of restaurants. Beers to look out for include Septem, Naxos, Siris, Solo, Seven Island and Athens' own Noctua.

▶ ATHENA'S COOK

🍴 20 Nikis – athenascook.gr – *daily 11.00-02.00*

Two blocks off Syntagma, this relaxed, family-run, open-fronted modern taverna is my favourite spot in the city for eating a broad menu of good modern Greek cooking alongside 20 beers from small, independent Greek breweries on a list twice that size. Up the way at No. 50 is an unusual beer shop called Brew Street (daily 12.00-23.30).

▶ BARLEY CARGO

🛈 6 Kolokotróni – FB/BarleyCargo – *daily 11.00-03.00*

With the feel of an upscale beach bar squeezed into a former carpet shop, this popular beer bar and grill is Athenian beer central, stocking up to 500 beers, of which around 200 are from Greece's 50 or so small independents. Not far from the National Historic Museum. Live music and beer festivals happen.

▶ BEERMAN

🛈 3 Agion Asomaton – bar-beerman.business.site – *daily 15.00-03.00*

This dark and broody, cavernous bar with a small terrace lies beyond the ancient Agora, not far from the Ceramics Museum. Expect 30 bottled Greek beers from a dozen breweries, plus imports from better-known Belgian, German and British independents. Food is salads, sandwiches, burgers or pizzas.

▶ BEERTIME

🛈 1 Plateia Iroon – FB/beertime.athens – *daily 16.00-01.00*

This cool-ish craft beer bar with a small terrace is found deep in a restaurant enclave off Athinas and Ermou. Beer focused, with food appearing at times, it has one of the best ranges of Greek beers in the city. For the very best, explorers need to find The Local Pub (25 Chaimanta – FB/thelocalpubathens) in chic, suburban Chalandrai, a fair walk from Aghia Paraskevi metro.

NEED TO KNOW

Avoid the prices and heat of high summer. The big sights are open year-round.

🛏 **Accommodation:** Stay in or near the centre in one of the limitless hotel or apartment options, which range from slick to basic.

🚌 **Getting around:** The best way to see the old centre is on foot. Walking is the quickest and easiest way to get round, with many backstreets pedestrianised and full of charm. Metred taxis are an affordable back-up for longer runs. Public transport is mostly for Athenians.

🍴 **Food:** Expect charcoal grills, slow roasts, cheese-and-tomato-stuffed vegetables, oregano-infused salads, and intense dips. Kebabs (souvlaki) are less common. Olives appear at breakfast. Be sure to sample at least one intensely sweet coffee, full of fine grounds.

✪ **Hints:** This is the edge of Europe, so some bars and restaurants allow smoking, drivers ignore seatbelts and many motorcyclists don't wear helmets. Tipping at 5-10% is appreciated.

ABOUT BAMBERG

Population: 77,000

Local breweries: Heller-Trum (Schlenkerla Aecht), Spezial, Fässla, Mahrs, Keesmann, Greifenklau and others in Bamberg; plus ± 200 small heritage breweries in the surrounding towns and villages of Oberfranken (Upper Franconia).

Trains: Bamberg station is near its centre and has direct connections with Berlin (±15 a day; 2.7-3.1 hours) and Hamburg (+9 a day; 4.7-5.1 hours); plus a one-change connection to Vienna (±6 a day; 5.1 hours).

Airport: Nuremburg airport currently has no direct connection with the UK. Transfer by U-bahn or train covers the 55km in 60-75 minutes and costs around €9 each way. A taxi booked in advance will cost ±€150. Munich airport is 2.6-3.2 hours away by train.

Currency: Euro (€)

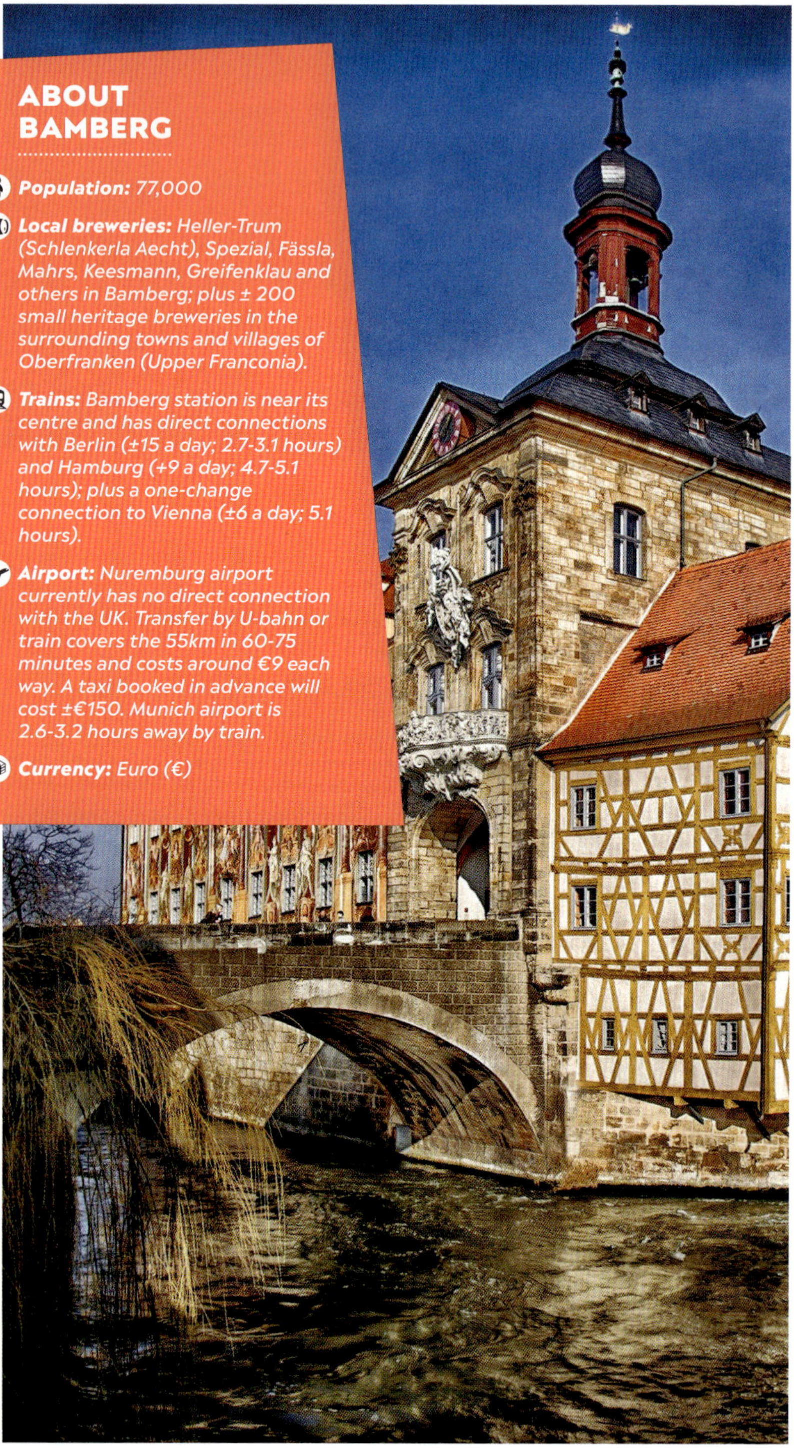

BAMBERG

Bamberg is draped across seven hills at the place where the river Regnitz meets the Main. In granting its Old Town a place on its World Heritage List in 1993, UNESCO cited the well-preserved and carefully restored early mediaeval layout, the baroque architecture and even the vineyards down the valley, but failed to mention its unique clutch of heritage breweries.

The world of beer owes more to this part of Bavaria than most people appreciate. Until recently it had more breweries per head of population than anywhere else and two of the beer styles these managed to preserve through the 20th century are unique pointers to beer's past.

Bamberg brewers are famed for using smoked malt to brew Rauchbier, a recipe choice that recalls the days when all beer was dark and smoky, before coke-fired ovens first allowed maltsters to produce paler and unsmoked malts.

Of even greater historical relevance, Kellerbier, literally 'cave beer', harks back to the days when some local brewers kept beer in cold mountain caves through hot summers to preserve it better, finding this also smoothed out some wrinkles in its flavour. These hazy, slightly earthy beers, best when racked unfiltered into an upright Holzfaß and served by gravity without added carbonation, are direct descendants of the first cold-conditioned beers, or 'lagers' if you prefer.

BEER VENUES

With few exceptions, Bamberg's taverns and inns tend to serve a narrow range of beers from one particular brewery, though with standard measures of 50cl, that is no bad thing. The nature of those breweries is what makes the beers special, and it is the old brewery taphouses that draw the beer tourists.

▶ BRAUEREI SPEZIAL

❶ ❽ Obere Königstraße 10
brauerei-spezial.de
Sa 09.00-02.00; others 09.00-22.30

This classically proportioned 475-year-old Bavarian inn houses a handful of bar rooms, a rear courtyard, a brewery and small maltings. Expect solid Franconian fayre to accompany delicate Rauchbier from home-smoked malt, Ungespundetes – the nearest lager gets to cask ale – and occasional specials. Bang opposite is the 370-year-old brewery and taphouse of equally essential Fässla (faessla.de – Su 08.30-12.00; others 08.30-23.00), and its lodgings.

▶ MAHRS BRÄU

🛈 🍽 **Wunderburg 10 – mahrs.de**
Su 10.00-15.00; Mo 15.00-23.00; others 11.00-22.00

Popular for its multiple rooms, dark wood and intimate atmosphere, the Mahrs taphouse has the broadest range of beers, with Ungespundetes the star of the show and Weißer Bock the winter wonder. Food has healthy and veggie options. Beyond the church, Keesmann Bräu (shut Su; Sa 09.30-15.00; others 10.30-22.30) is famed for its crystal-clear Helles, its scrub-top tables, sound menu and commercial reticence.

▶ SCHLENKERLA

🛈 🍽 **Dominikaner Straße 6**
schlenkerla.de – daily 09.30-23.30

The Heller-Trum brewery is located up the hill, a way from its historic taphouse in the old centre. It can get rammed at obvious times so go off peak. The ancient snug bar is by unwritten invitation only, but the smoked Märzen is good everywhere, served straight from the Holzfaß with seasonal specials, trumping a pretty solid, well-presented food offer.

▶ BRAUEREI GREIFENKLAU

🛈 🍽 **Laurenziplatz 20**
greifenklau.de – shut Su-Mo; Sa 11.00-22.30; others 15.00-22.30

Bamberg's oldest taphouse is for me up there with the best. A bracing walk, halfway up one of the city's many hills, rewards with a good view from the beer garden. The inside is plainer than the others but all the more authentic for that. Its four beers are joined by a Bock in winter and Rauchbier in summer and the kitchen works all day till 20.30.

▶ ABSEITS

🛈 🍽 **Podeldorferstraße 39**
abseits-bamberg.de – daily from 17.00, plus Sa-Su 09.00-14.00

To get this timeless beer café, understand its name. In football abseits means off-side, in other contexts outside, apart, or distant. On the other side of the train tracks from the city, its 100-strong beer list is strongest on small independent Franconian breweries. The weekend breakfasts are legendary. By day it's salads, soups, baguettes and TexMex.

ABSEITS

▶ BIEROTHEK

📍 Unterer Königstraße 1
bierothek.de/stores/Bamberg – *shut Su; Fr-Sa 10.00-20.00; others 11.00-19.00*

Over 75% of beer in Germany is bought from shops so it is hardly surprising that chains of specialist beer stores like Bierothek have sprung up, selling 500+ beers of every style and tradition, including in recent years ones not made in Germany. Do your research before entering or madness will descend. They will ship to anywhere in the EU.

NEED TO KNOW

Enjoying the home of the equally world-famous Weyermann's maltings and brewery maker Kasper Schulz, a beer museum (Michelsberg 10f; Apr-Oct) and even a small hop garden (Zollnerstrasse 24) will easily fill three days, but consider staying longer to explore brewhouses found a bus ride away in Geisfeld, Roßdorf, Memmelsdorf and Merkedorf, or the 20+ Bierkellers of the Kellerwald, just up the track near Forchheim.

🛏 **Accommodation:** The problem with UNESCO World Heritage Sites is that they rarely have cheap hotels, though from mid-October to Easter prices here are standard European. The top pick is always the much-clicked, timber-framed Nepomuk, perched above the fast-flowing Regnitz, now with Eckerts beer bar. The Spezial and Fässla breweries have rooms too.

🚌 **Getting around:** The city is easily traversed on foot, fortunately as there is no U-bahn, S-bahn or tram system here. Buses go all over the region, with tickets at €2.10 each or €7.20 for 4; and day-passes €4.70 per person or €7.60 for up to 6 travelling together. A whole week pass for up to six is €15.20.

🍴 **Food:** Typical Bavarian fayre means pork, dumplings, sauerkraut and rye bread. Local variants include Blaue Zipfel (blue-tinged sausages), roasted Schäuferla (pork shoulder on the bone), or mince options like Bamberger Zwiebeln (stuffed onions) and Krautbraten (baked cabbage with onion). Hörnla are traditional local croissants.

⭐ **Hints:** Tipping involves mostly rounding up, with extra for exceptional service. They call it Trinkgeld, or literally 'drink money'.

ABOUT BARCELONA

- **Population:** City 1,620,000; metropolitan area 5,640,000

- **Local breweries:** Garage, Fort, Edge, Barcelona, Oddity, Freddo Fox and a dozen others (craft), plus twice that number of brand purveyors posing as brewers.

- **Trains:** Centrally located Barcelona Sants station has direct connections with Madrid (±30 a day; 2.5-3.2 hours); Algeciras, for Gibraltar (2 a day; 17 hours); and Paris (1 a day; 6.8 hours), plus one-change connections to Bordeaux (2 a day; 7 hours).

- **Airport:** Barcelona El Prat airport is at the city's southern limits and has direct connections with London Heathrow, Gatwick, Stansted and eight regional airports. The Aerobús between each terminal and Plaça Catalunya runs every 5-10 minutes, takes half an hour and costs €5.90 single, €10.20 return. Metro L9 is better for the University. All are covered by the Hola Barcelona card (see Need to know). A taxi will cost €35-40 each way.

- **Ferry port:** Ferries between Barcelona and Civitavecchia, 40km from Rome (20 hours), sail a couple of times a week

- **Currency:** Euro (€)

BEER BREAKS

BARCELONA

Ten years ago, if a mate suggested you go to Spain for a few beers you could be pretty confident that they had a laddish trip in mind. Nowadays, in Barcelona at least, you will find a beer scene to take on all-comers. If you like the idea of enjoying every style of bar and beer there is, and eating what you like when you like, BCN is the place for you.

Barcelona is the capital city of Catalonia (Catalunya). Although part of Spain, most locals identify as Catalan, and speak a language as different from Spanish as Portuguese. The regional politics display a quietly determined separatist spirit that other young Spaniards often respect but the Spanish political class despises.

Having no indigenous beer style means that all are fair game, for importation, imitation and rule-changing. The idea that chilled Imperial Stout is a suitable bevvy for a late summer's evening is not considered daft – after all, Rioja works.

The city's biggest tourist draw is the magnificent whimsy of architect Antoni Gaudí and his fellow Modernistas. You can spend hours on board BusTurístico spotting heritage sites and neighbourhoods you could explore. If time allows only one, make it La Sagrada Familia, Gaudí's still evolving basilica – Christendom's grooviest church and one of the world's most memorable buildings.

BEER VENUES

Spain is Europe's third largest producer of beer, after Germany and Poland: Cruzcampo is Heineken; Mahou, though Spanish, is linked to Filipino giant San Miguel; and Damm, as in Estrella, is from Barcelona. Since 2009 Spain has grown 600+ new breweries, roughly half in Catalonia, equalling the growth rate of Italy and France. Local and regional beers are everywhere and the city has maybe 80+ specialist beer bars, of which these give just a flavour.

▶ GARAGE UNIVERSITAT

❶ ⑪ Carrer Consell de Cent 261 – garagebeer.co
Sa-Su 16.00-24.00; Mo-Fr 17.00-24.00 – metro: Universitat L1 & L2 (400m)

Originally designed as an ubercool brewpub, Garage Beer Co outgrew these premises in 2017, though they still use some fermentation vessels behind the glass. Now a taphouse with tapas – light but enough to keep you there – it serves around a dozen immaculate Garage beers, which included, on my last visit, the best cask Porter of my sampling year.

GARAGE UNIVERSITAT

▶ BIERCAB
🚪🍺🍽 **Carrer de Muntaner 55 – biercab.com** - *shut Su; Mo-Sa 12.00-24.00 – metro L1, L2: Universitat*

Unusually, few of the beers in this elegant bar are Catalan or Spanish but their ability to spot brewers and brands of the future, and source them on draught, is remarkable. The bottled list has a huge number of collectibles, at a price. The tapas are, in contrast, more reliable than eye-opening. A shop (Mo-Sa 15.30-22.00) opened during COVID.

▶ EL VASO DE ORO
🍺🍽 **Carrer de Balboa 6 – vasodeoro.com** *daily 12.00-24.00 – metro L4: Barceloneta*

Ironically, in this city of a thousand beers, the one must-do bar stocks mostly the local Fort brewery's range. What it does better than anywhere is tapas. Use patience or luck to nab a stool somewhere along its elongated bar top, then eye the passing plates until you spot something you fancy matching with a flute of your next beer style.

▶ BEER'LINALE
🍺🍽 **Carrer del Carme 7 – beerlinale.com** *Fr-Sa 11.00-01.00; Su-Th 11.00-24.00 – metro L3: Liceu*

Just short of posh, toned down by bare-brick walls and scrub-top tables, there is something self-assured about this place. Within the extensive list of rare and special beers, with some collectors' items at eye-watering prices, is a more restrained list of contemporary stuff, supported by a tapas menu that promotes the Mediterranean diet.

▶ ABIRRADERO
🍺🍽 **Carrer de Vila I Vila 77 – abirradero.com** *Sa-Su from 12.00; Mo-Fr from 18.00 – metro L2, L3: Paral-lel*

This no frills, sidestreet brewpub off Paral-lel sells its own beers and many others from breweries that belong to Catalonia's Institute of Craft Brewers. Its seats dribble onto the street even when it hosts live jazz. The tapas and burgers are really a sideshow. Tends to close around midnight, or 01.00 at weekends.

NEED TO KNOW

Barcelona is open for visiting all year round, though July to early September can be unpleasantly hot and crowded. Barcelona Beer Festival (see European Beer Events Calendar page 33) is one of the very best.

Accommodation: Prices are at the cheaper end of the European norm and hotels and apartments of all standards are widely available. The most central location for public transport is the area around Plaça de Catalunya.

Getting around: Five companies vie for bus, tram, metro and local rail services, collaboration is limited and signage could be better. To cut through this buy a Hola Barcelona card (holabarcelona.com) for 48 (€16.40), 72 (€23.80), 96 (€31) or 120 (€38.20) hours, which includes the airport connections. Uber, Mytaxi and Cabify all operate in the city.

Food: The forte of many Spanish regions is tapas and Catalunya is no exception. Graze, don't binge is the order of the day. An infinite variety of tasty morsels should support and complement your beer, not get in its way.

Hints: Tipping is not expected and can occasionally cause insult. Don't jaywalk unless the locals are. Many city maps are 45° off kilter.

LAMBICUS

▶ LAMBICUS

🛈 🍴 🍺 Carrer de Tamarit 107 – lambicus.com *Sa-Su 12.00-23.00, Mo-Fr 17.00-23.00 – metro L3: Poble Sec*

Younger Catalan beer lovers travelling abroad brought back beers, stories and sometimes whole business concepts, such as this distinctly Flemish ale house, with an extraordinary beer selection that would shine in any Belgian city. There are light tapas too. Its shop around the corner (Carrer Rocafort 9 – Tu-Sa 12.00-14.00 Tu-Fr 17.00-20.00) stocks 400.

ABIRRADERO

BARCELONA 55

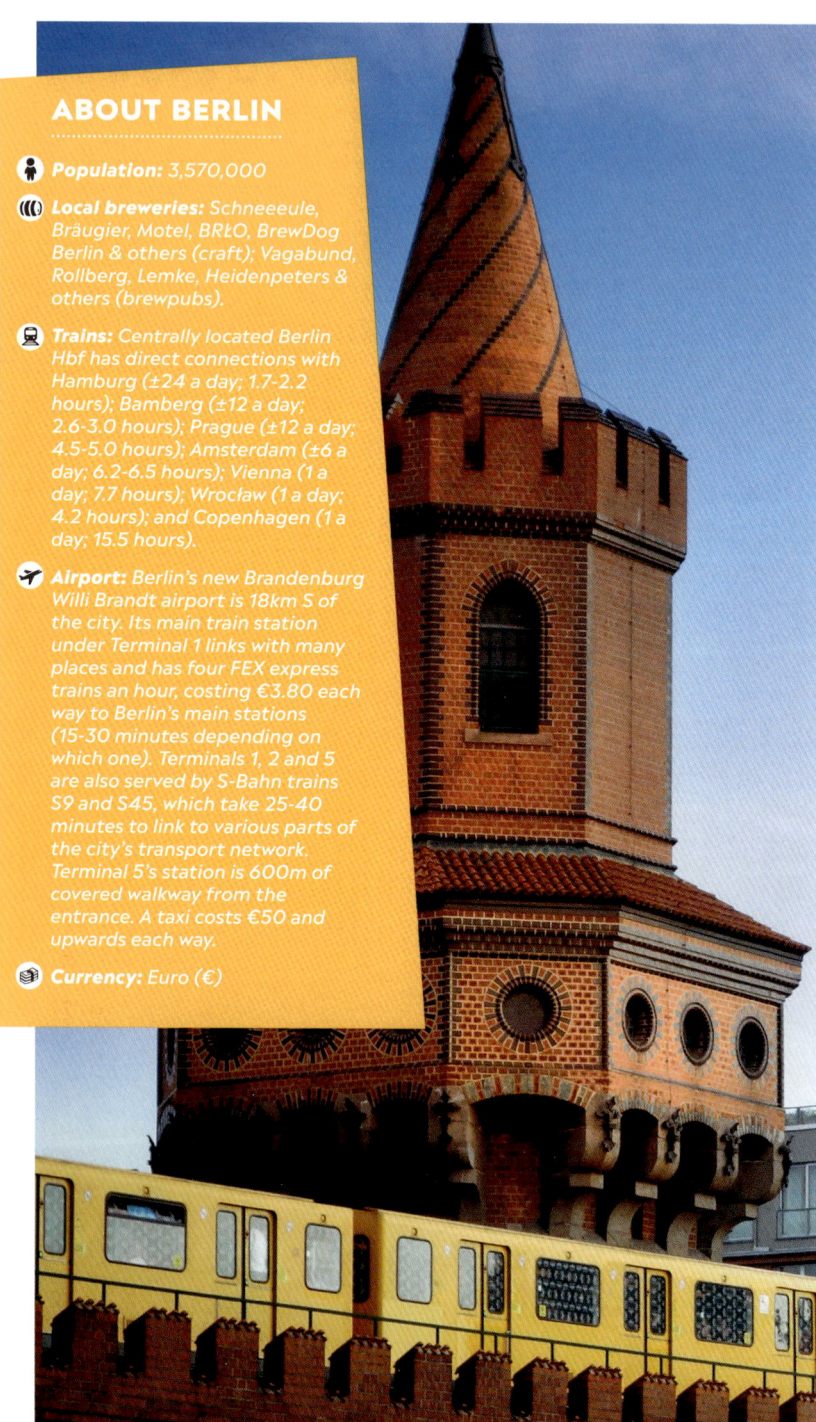

ABOUT BERLIN

Population: 3,570,000

Local breweries: Schneeeule, Bräugier, Motel, BRŁO, BrewDog Berlin & others (craft); Vagabund, Rollberg, Lemke, Heidenpeters & others (brewpubs).

Trains: Centrally located Berlin Hbf has direct connections with Hamburg (±24 a day; 1.7-2.2 hours); Bamberg (±12 a day; 2.6-3.0 hours); Prague (±12 a day; 4.5-5.0 hours); Amsterdam (±6 a day; 6.2-6.5 hours); Vienna (1 a day; 7.7 hours); Wrocław (1 a day; 4.2 hours); and Copenhagen (1 a day; 15.5 hours).

Airport: Berlin's new Brandenburg Willi Brandt airport is 18km S of the city. Its main train station under Terminal 1 links with many places and has four FEX express trains an hour, costing €3.80 each way to Berlin's main stations (15-30 minutes depending on which one). Terminals 1, 2 and 5 are also served by S-Bahn trains S9 and S45, which take 25-40 minutes to link to various parts of the city's transport network. Terminal 5's station is 600m of covered walkway from the entrance. A taxi costs €50 and upwards each way.

Currency: Euro (€)

BERLIN

British beer drinkers associate Germany with pale lagers in the same way that German tourists associate Britain with instant coffee. In each case the idea is a decade or two out of date. The Berlin beer scene today is about all kinds of beer, with clear, blond and frothy-topped varieties struggling more than they should in a maelstrom of influences from across Europe and North America.

For three decades before November 1989 Berliners were less concerned by beer than with a snake-like abomination, built out of concrete and fear, called the Berlin Wall. It appeared one weekend in August 1961 to keep 'the West' from influencing the post-War Russian empire. Its presence lives on in the city's absence of a real central area, Alexanderplatz being the bustling heart of old East Berlin and Kurfürstendamm the overly fashioned West.

Behind this lie centuries of history, in a capital city that has a bad case of Imposter Syndrome – never feeling as grand or permanent as Europe's others. From 1451 to 1918 it was the seat of power of the Electors of Brandenburg, later to become the German Kaisers, via a time as Kings of Prussia. Successive rulers were obsessed with military dominance, gorgeous palaces, large green spaces and elegant squares, and by steady acquisition they gathered the 300+ minor German-speaking states for eventual unification in 1871, under Bismarck.

Berlin has no Gothic cathedrals or Graeco-Roman sites. What it does have is the architectural legacy of Karl Friedrich Schinkel, the 19th century designer of the Lustgarten, the Tiergarten, the Konzerthaus on Gendarmenmarkt, the Altes Museum on Museuminsel, and Neue Wache guardhouse on Unter den Linden, all of which survived the 1939-45 war, after which 90% of the city lay in ruins. Few trees are more than 80 years old.

BEER VENUES

There might be 400 places in Berlin where taking a beer could be fun. As befits a city with no single downtown area, great beer bars are found in the oddest of places. While German-made craft beers and US imports are trending, heritage styles from many countries are often found in this most cosmopolitan of European beer destinations. By choosing a handful I have tried to give a feel of the breadth of experience available.

MUTED HORN

▶ FOERSTERS FEINE BIER

🛈 🍴 Bornstraße 20 - foerstersfeinebier.de – *shut Su-Mo; Tu-Sa 17.00-23.00 – U9: Walther-Schreiber-Platz*

Some people don't get this place. They find it too simple, not aimed at craft beer geeks. Instead, it gathers together a mostly German array of beers from all genres and serves them up in a neat, unrushed, neighbourhood beer bar with small terrace. The snacks are light bites from the traditional Berliner cookbook. My favourite bar in all Berlin.

▶ MUTED HORN

🛈 🍺 🍴 Flughafenstraße 49 - themutedhorn.com
Sa-Su 17.00-03.00; others 17.00-02.00 – U8: Boddinstraße

In sharp contrast to the last entry is this bare-walled, scrub-tabled, top-ranking craft beer bar I try hard to hate but fail. Its initial love of beers with too much haze, sweetener or inept acidity has evolved into a superb list of 20+ top rate draughts and over a hundred bottles and cans, now also available to go. No food but you may bring your own.

▶ MONTEREY

🛈 Danziger Straße 61
- montereybar.com
daily from 17.00 – U2: Eberswalder Straße

I am too old for this dark and noisy place but you may not be. Its shabbiness is

studied, the ten taps and bottle-can list almost too clever, and music more for tolerating than hearing, but I go for the one and usually end up having three. Stays open past midnight. No food.

HOPFENREICH

Sorauer Straße 31 – hopfenreich.de
daily from 16.00 – U1: Schlesisches Tor

Often crowded in the evenings but with something about it at quieter times that exudes a certain charm. It's probably the battered wooden look, the chuck-away wall decorations and the candles. The range of 20+ draught beers is carefully chosen and ever-changing but take a look at the bottles too. If they still do pickled sausage, try it.

HOPFENREICH

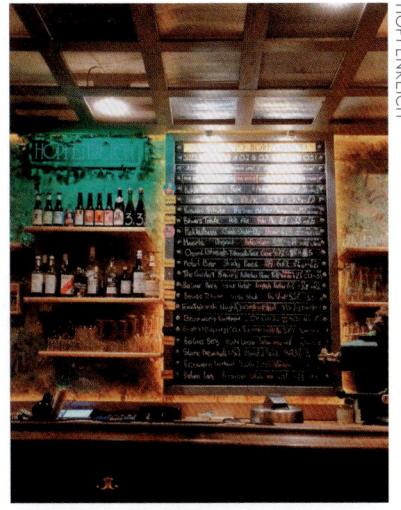

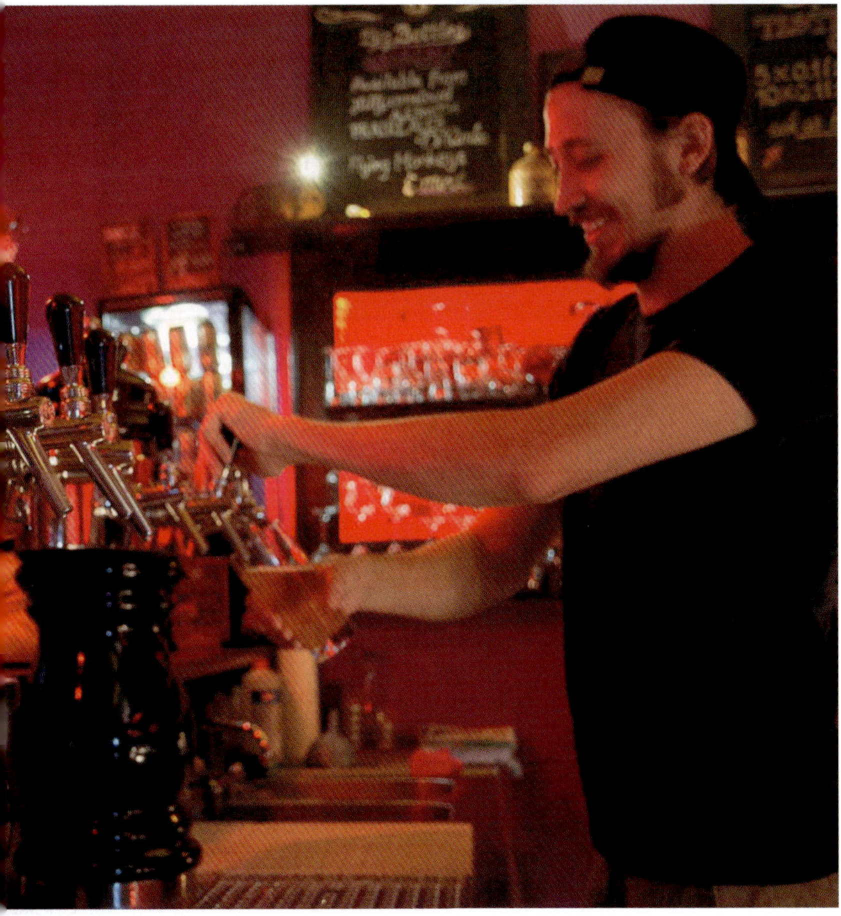

MONTEREY

BIRRA

🛈 🍴 **Prenzlauer Allee 198 – FB/birraberlin** - *shut Mo; Tu-Su from 18.00 – U2: Eberswalder Straße*

It is hard to believe that this beautifully absurd place has thrived right from the word go. Owned by one of Italy's oldest craft breweries, Lambrate, almost all of the ±100 beers served here are Italian, including the three on handpull. There is good, light Italian snacking to be had too. Closes around midnight, or later at weekends.

BIEREREI BAR & VINTAGE CELLAR

🛈 **Oranienstraße 185 – FB/bierereibar**
Sa-Su from 14.00; Mo-Fr from 16.00 – U1, U3, U8: Kottbusser Tor

Unique and classy specialist beer bar and sampling cellar in Kreuzberg. This is where you come to try the special beers you are unlikely to find elsewhere. A good eclectic mix of traditional and modern German, plus selected imports, with conversation tending to centre on beer a lot. No food or other distractions.

GETRÄNKEFEINKOST

🛈 **Boxhagener Straße 24 – getraenkefeinkost.de**
shut Su; Sa 11.00-20.00; others 13.00-20.00 – U5: Frankfurter Tor

This neat beer shop is part of a small chain stocking a wide range of German craft and heritage beers, plus a goodly range of Belgian, British and others. Across the street from Protokoll (protokollberlin.de – Mo-Fr from 17.00; Sa-Su from 16.00), a craft taproom from central casting that has interesting Russian beers among its 20+ taps and 100+ bottle-cans.

▶ BRŁO BRWHOUSE

🚪 🍴 Schönberger Straße 16 – en.brlo.de
*shut Mo; Sa-Su 12.00-24.00; Tu-Fr
14.00-24.00 – U1, U2, U3: Gleisdreieck*

This all-singing, all-dancing, community-supporting, sustainability-driven, craft brewery taphouse and restaurant is made from 28 shipping containers, making it one of the weirder looking bars in Europe. The summer terrace has deckchairs and hop bines. The must-book restaurant majors on vegetable dishes but caters well for carnivores.

Other places to drink include **Augustiner am Gendarmenmarkt** (Charlottenstraße 55 – daily 10.00-01.00 – U6: **Französischestraße**, U2: Hausvogteiplatz) for old-fashioned grandeur, Bavarian food and Holzfass tapping at 18.00; **Heidenpeters** (Markthalle Neun, Eisenbahnstraße – shut Su-Mo; Th 12.00-22.00; others 12.00-20.00 – U1, U3: Görlitzer Bahnhof) for taproom drinking in a foody market stall brewpub; **Vagabund** (Antwerpenerstraße 3 – Sa-Su from 13.00; others from 17.00 – U6: Seestraße) for steady craft brews in the city's nicest brewpub; and **Lager Lager** (Pflugerstraße 68 – shut Su; Sa from 12.00; others from 14.00 – U8: Schönleinstraße) for great take-home beers and a shabby chic tasting room.

VAGABUND

NEED TO KNOW

Berlin makes London look slick. Its infrastructure still harks back to its time as two prized cities of different empires. Just wandering around and hoping to find something entertaining doesn't work. As befits the capital city of a nation of orderly folk, plan your days and your routes, and if anything interesting crops up on the way, see it as a bonus.

🛏 **Accommodation:** Central Berlin is awash with hotels and apartments, though most are functional rather than beautiful. Prices are seasonal and advance bookings can save you heavily. For the best transport connections aim to stay in Mitte, or around either Friedrichstraße or Alexanderplatz.

🚇 **Getting around:** Public transport in Berlin may appear random but is highly organised (berlin.de). The S-Bahn, U-Bahn, trams, buses and ferries all share the same tickets. Ticket machines everywhere sell single fares for €3-3.80 depending on which zones are crossed; 4 for €9.40-13.80. A 24-hour card is €8.80-10, or €25.50-26.50 for groups of up to 5; 7 day is €36-43; and a month is €86-107. Travelling without a ticket costs €60 on the spot and you won't talk or weep your way out of it.

🍴 **Food:** Classic local pub food still features variations on pork, ham, potatoes, sour-cooked cabbage and mustards, though you can find all types of food in Berlin's many thousands of snack bars, cafés, bistros and restaurants. Vegan and green are trending heavily.

⭐ **Hints:** Tipping is not obligatory, though 'keep the change' is appreciated, and 5 to 10% in restaurants is now commonplace.

BERLIN 61

ABOUT BOLOGNA

Population: City 366,000; urban area 810,000

Local brewers: Ca' del Brado, Zapap and others.

Trains: Bologna Centrale station is on the heptagonal ring of dual carriageways that encircle the city centre. It has direct connections with Rome (±100 a day; 2.0-2.5 hours).

Airport: Bologna Marconi airport is 6km NW of the city and has direct flights to/from Heathrow; Luton; Manchester; and Stansted. The Marconi Express elevated shuttle to Centrale departs 8 times an hour, takes 7 minutes and costs €9.20 one way, €17 return. A taxi costs €20-25 and is usually much slower.

Currency: Euro (€)

BOLOGNA

If you want to explore and understand northern Italy by visiting a single place, go to Bologna. A city of colonnades and modern art, of downpours and dry curing, designed with people rather than chain stores or cars in mind. It is home to Maserati, Lamborghini, Ferrari, Ducati and the Slow Food movement. Its claim to be the food capital of one of the world's best-blessed food cultures is not immodest. In this city of gourmands expect to drink, dine and relax well.

Bologna is the largest city in Emilia Romagna region, at the centre of a fertile plain where fruit trees, grain and vegetables grow in vast profusion and where Italy's nascent hop farms are based. Cities like Verona, Modena and Ravenna make an easy day out by train – even Florence or Venice if you make an early start.

It has been a joy to watch the Italian beer scene grow from a counter-intuitive notion to a burgeoning industry, at every stage growing yet more of the skills to produce classic beer styles and then branch out into new ones.

BEER VENUES

Little over a decade ago, it would have been impossible to find a specialist bar in the city. The early days of birra artigianale (literally 'craft' or 'artisanal' beer) saw brewers aiming their beers at the restaurant sector, a fact still reflected in the routine stocking of a few local beers in most restaurants. But as times change, so more is possible.

➤ ASTRAL BEERS PUB

🛈 🍴 Via Castiglione 13B – FB/astralbeerspub – *shut Su; Sa 18.00-01.00; others 12.30-15.00 & 18.00-24.00 (Fr 01.00)*

Plain but elegant, smallish beer bar near Guastavillani Palace. Nine taps include one handpull, plus ±80 bottles. The list majors on Italy, Belgium and the UK, with a cleverly chosen smattering from elsewhere in Europe. For the Bolognese version of a pie and a pint take one of the bruschetta and beer options. Beer is available for take-home too.

ASTRAL BEERS PUB

▶ RANZANI 13

🛈 🍴 Via Camilio Ranzani 5/12 – pizzeriaranzani13.it – *daily 19.00-01.00, plus Mo-Fr 12.00-14.30*

Set among apartment blocks just outside the inner ring, the twin attractions at this ground-floor café are the well-picked ranges of Belgian and Italian beers, plus the finest slow-fermented sourdough pizza and calzone in the world, according to some normally restrained judges. The 70+ beer list consists mostly of classics. There is a small satellite version in the Mercato delle Erbe.

▶ LORTICA

🛈 🍴 Via Mascarella 26B – lortica.org – *Sa & Su 17.00-01.30; others 14.00-01.30*

Popular with students on term time evenings, this long bar with a large back room is best appreciated at quieter times. Find it in the colonnaded recesses near the Odeon cinema, likely behind an impromptu terrace. Good small snacks supplement a sound range of ±60 bottles and a dozen draughts, not always advertised.

▶ MADAMA BEERSTRÒ

🛈 🍴 Via San Vitali 31 – madamabeerstro.it – *shut Su; others 17.30 till late*

A bright and breezy beer bar under the portici, a five-minute walk from Piazza Maggiore, against the traffic on an arterial road. The centre of attention is its ten beers on tap, though the near-hidden selection of ±70 bottles and cans have more of interest. Nice nibbles and a variety of snacks are enough to make a tapas-like meal.

▶ IL PUNTO

🛈 🍴 Via San Rocco 1 – puntobologna.com – *daily 17.30-01.30*

The epitome of a great Italian beer café. In its open bar and streetside verandah you will find many and varied beers on tap, often including a handpulled Italian ale, plus a huge range of fresh and vintage bottles, including among the Italian specials several of Baladin's pan-flat 14% Xyauyù Barley Wine range. The kitchen does enough to sustain.

MADAMA BEERSTRÒ

▶ LA TANA DEL LUPPULO

Via Luigi Calori 3 – latanadellluppulo.info – *daily 17.30-01.30*

Bologna's first serious beer bar moved its base to the corner of the square in 2019 to this well-lit, street-corner bar and restaurant, also badged as Draft & Dreams. The vibe is casual, though intentions are serious, the specialties here being handpicked Italian, Belgian and other beers, with up to 20 on draught and over 60 in bottle, plus a food offer that is almost as complicated and delicious.

▶ IL PRETESTO

Via Riva di Reno 68 – beershopbologna.it – *shut Su; others 11.00-13.00 & 15.00-18.00*

Although COVID prompted quite a few bars to increase their take-away and delivery orders, the best bet in Bologna for take-home is this small shop with ±400 beers from ±80 breweries, a dozen of which are Italian, with the rest mostly European. The emphasis is on classical brews, as befits a city obsessed with aromas and flavours.

NEED TO KNOW

The Eataly chain of food shops and restaurants promotes the values of the Slow Food movement, which helped to lead the backlash against the industrialisation of food and drink. In what may appear a contradiction in terms, the 100,000m^2 theme park called FICO, on the outskirts of town, houses 40 producers including a Baladin-owned brewery. Reach it by bus F from opposite Central Station.

Accommodation: There are hotels and apartments everywhere but try to stay within the heptagon of dual carriageways that make up the inner ring. If you intend to tour a bit, staying on the station side makes sense. Prices vary with the season, though the city's many attractions are open year-round.

Getting around: The tiny streets of the old centre around Piazza Maggiore can only be explored on foot, while spreading out from the centre are 40km of colonnaded pavements, or portici, offering excellent protection from sun and rain and likely your abiding memory of a beautiful city. Buses cost €1.50 for a single end-to-end trip, (€1.30 in advance), or €5 a day, but walking is more fun.

Food: The cluster of food specialists in and around the Mercato delle Erbe on Via Ugo Bassi is a good place to start, while pick 'n' mix browsing is possible at shared tables in the Mercato di Mezzo on Via Clavature, which includes a bar from top Italian brewery Baladin.

Hints: Tipping in bars and restaurants involves rounding up, though it can buy love from hotel staff. Italians handle alcohol well. Drunks are few and far between and mostly foreign.

ABOUT BORDEAUX

Population: Municipality 240,000; metropolitan area 990,000

Local breweries: Azimut, Bordeaux Beer Factory and others.

Trains: Bordeaux Saint-Jean station is a major hub in the south of the centre and has direct connections with Paris (±16 a day; 2.1-3.5 hours), plus one-change connection to Barcelona (2 a day; 7 hours).

Airport: Bordeaux airport, at Mérignac on the western outskirts of the city, has direct connections with Gatwick, Stansted and Manchester. Until the tram A line extension to the airport is finished, links with the St Jean station in the centre rely on the once or twice hourly 30'D Direct bus, which takes 30 minutes and costs €8 each way, or the hour-long but more frequent Lianne 1 bus, which costs €1.70. Each uses Terminal B. Taxis or Uber cost up to €50 each way.

Currency: Euro (€)

BORDEAUX

The city of Bordeaux, on France's Atlantic coast, midway down the Bay of Biscay, near to where the river Garonne meets the sea, is the centre of perhaps the most famous wine region in Europe, though its beer scene is also worth exploring.

It is a little-known fact that the city hosts the HQ of the world's eighth largest and arguably most reclusive brewery company, Groupe Castel, responsible for producing 40 million hl of beer a year, mostly in Africa. Its profile in the city is near non-existent, however, as it represents only a small part of the mostly privately-owned group's global wine business, which markets an astonishing 34 million hl of wine to the world each year.

The simplest sightseeing opportunity is to take a lengthy promenade along the west bank of the Garonne as it scythes through the city, starting near the Gare St. Jean and heading north (downstream). This takes you past the Bourse and Opéra National, with optional side trips to the Gothic Cathedral of St André and its climbable Pey Berland bell tower, and the CAPC modern art museum.

Striding further will offer the opportunity to add visits to the august Musée du Vin et du Négoce and the far flashier Cité du Vin, each of which may assist your understanding of how it is that I came to believe that wine is so much simpler than beer.

BEER VENUES

The word that best sums up the Bordeaux beer scene is 'individual'. There are few examples of off-the-peg craft beer bars here, maybe because beer has had to try so hard to impact. The businesses that have thrived are far more made-to-measure.

▶ JAQEN

🛈🍺 5 Rue Beaubadat – jaqencraftbeer.com – *shut Su; Mo-Th 16.30-23.00; Fr-Sa 14.30-23.00 – tram B: Gambetta*

Primarily a beer shop in theory but the simple beauty and comfort of its counter and service area means it enjoys as much popularity as a beer bar. Warm and friendly with knowledgeable servers, its list extends to a dozen taps and hundreds of bottles-cans, grouped to style. Spin-off restaurant bar Jaqen Tuki (117bis Cours Victor Hugo – jaqentuki.com) adds clever food, deletes most bottles and swaps atmosphere for style.

▶ LE ZYTHO

🛈🍽 28 Rue Latour – lezytho.fr – *daily from 17.30 – tram B; CAPC Musée d'Art*

Unquestionably a cave and small terrace aimed at those who already get beer, its active focus being entirely on giving

LES BERTHOM

French and other small independent breweries a fair crack at the market. Around 15 beers on tap and over 100 on the shelves are supplemented by a decent array of tasty snacks, sufficient to keep you there without stealing the show.

▶ LES BERTHOM

🛈 45 Cours d'Alsace-et-Lorraine – lesberthom.com – *Sa-Su from 16.00; Mo-Fr from 17.00 – tram A: Place du Palais*

Two hundred metres off the quay, near Pont de Pierre. Having said that Bordeaux beer places are individual, this one is part of a national chain of 16 bars that showcase a sizable number of French and foreign beers, always including the Belgian Duvel Moortgat range. The staff here are attentive, making it a pleasant stop to while away a part of the evening.

▶ LA BIÈRISTERIE

🛈🍴 6 Rue Porte de Cailhou – labieristerie.com – *shut Su-Mo; Tu-Sa from 17.00 – tram A: Place du Palais*

Not the loudest or most obviously trending beer café in the part of the centre entered from the quay via the Cailhou city gate, but the best designed. The shortish beer list is mostly class stuff with a lot of French independents. The menu of accompanying snacks is also well put together.

▶ MILLE ET UNE BIÈRES BORDEAUX

🛈🍴 42 Rue Edmond Besse – mille-et-une-bieres.fr – *shut Su; Mo-Tu 13.30-20.00; We-Sa 10-20.00 – tram B: Berges de la Garonne*

It is easy for the beer tourist to form inaccurate opinions of a place by experiencing only its centre. To avoid this in

Bordeaux, take tram B to its northern terminal, then walk ten minutes down Edmond Besse to find this huge, basic beer hall and shop, serving and selling over 1,000 beers, a few from Azimut brewery, which you will pass on the way.

▶ L'AMIRALE BIÈRE

🔒 5 Rue Saint-James – lamiraledebiere.fr – shut Su; Mo 15.00-19.00; Tu-Sa 11.00-13.30; 15.00-19.00) – tram A: Sainte-Catherine

Not a beer shop that stocks infinite variety but rather one run with intelligence and focus, its aim to 'convince the sceptics, please the curious, share with the convinced and satisfy the epicurean'. Hence, it also carries a neat range of nibbles and spreads to go with six-packs of local, classic or just plain unusual beers, from a range of 250 or so.

NEED TO KNOW

Like much of France, Bordeaux downsizes considerably in August, when it can also be stiflingly hot, while its proximity to the Bay of Biscay means it rains roughly half the year – a great combination if you are a grape vine.

🛏 **Accommodation:** The most popular location is on the west bank of the river between St. Jean station and Pont Jacques Chaban Delmas, though quality varies and prices change with what's on in the wine world. Alternatives are the east bank or anywhere on the main tram lines.

🚌 **Getting around:** The airport aside, Bordeaux has an incredibly efficient, fast and reliable tram, bus and river shuttle network (infotbm.fr), which is fully integrated and easy-to-follow. Tickets valid for 60 minutes cost €1.70 for 1, €3 for 2 and €13.20 for 10; or else €2.60 for a night out (19.00-07.00), €5 for 24 hours and €14.20 for 7 days.

🍽 **Food:** If you have in mind to take light lunches and heavier dinners in lovely traditional bistros or small family-run restaurants found by chance, serving specialities of the region, either think again or else do some careful advance planning that involves reservations. Les fast foods internationaux have taken root and flourish ici.

⭐ **Hints:** Tipping is considered a sign of being embarrassed or English-speaking. Street corner bars serving a glass of red have largely gone, so to take wine without mushing your wallet try Aux 4 Coins du Vin (8 Rue de la Devise – aux4coinsduvin.com – tram C, D: Place de la Bourse).

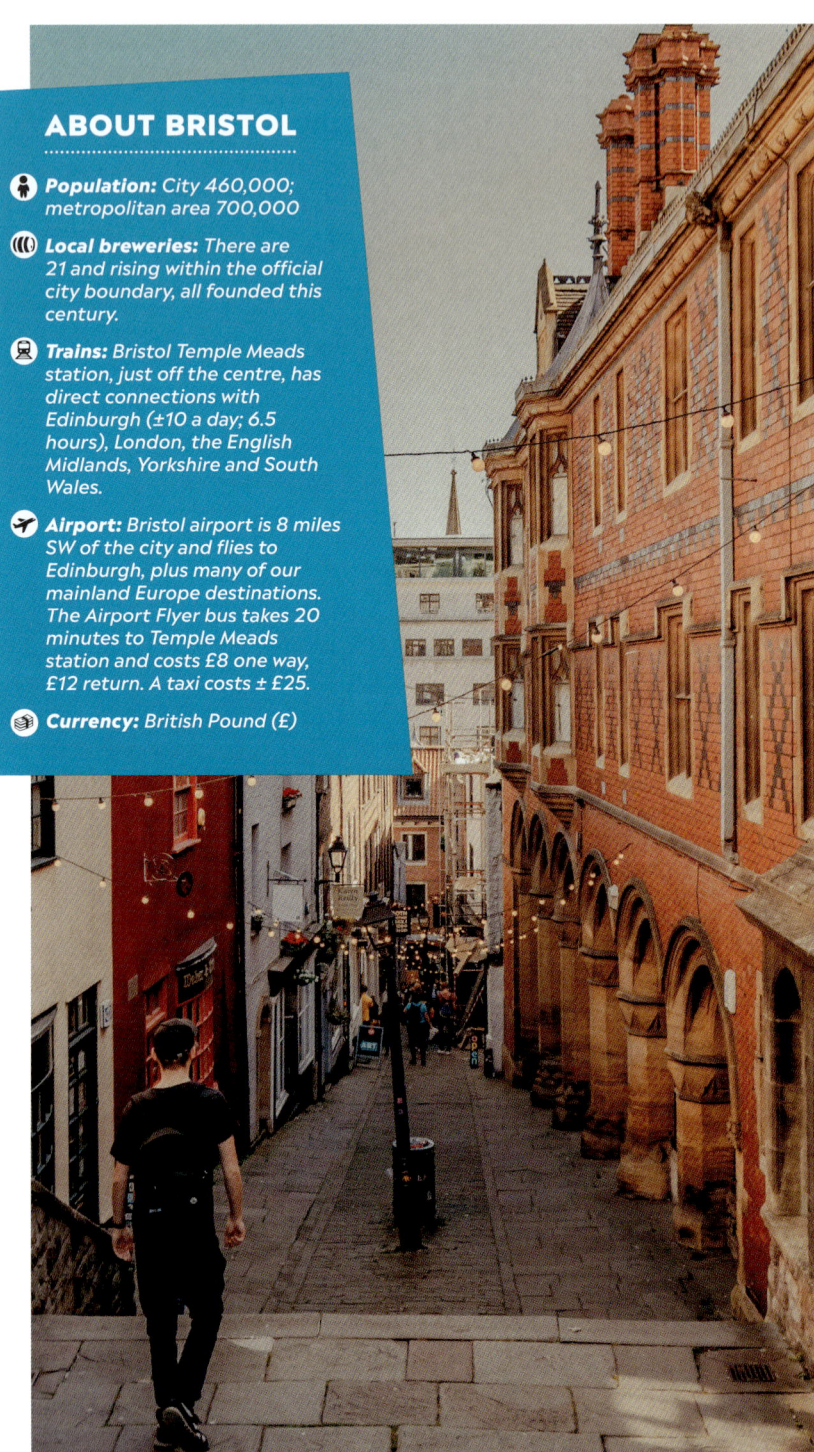

ABOUT BRISTOL

- **Population:** City 460,000; metropolitan area 700,000
- **Local breweries:** There are 21 and rising within the official city boundary, all founded this century.
- **Trains:** Bristol Temple Meads station, just off the centre, has direct connections with Edinburgh (±10 a day; 6.5 hours), London, the English Midlands, Yorkshire and South Wales.
- **Airport:** Bristol airport is 8 miles SW of the city and flies to Edinburgh, plus many of our mainland Europe destinations. The Airport Flyer bus takes 20 minutes to Temple Meads station and costs £8 one way, £12 return. A taxi costs ± £25.
- **Currency:** British Pound (£)

BRISTOL

Having been accused all my life of being Bristolian, for a lilt in my much-travelled accent, 2015 saw fate land me here. Within two years, the City of Bristol had become the most brewery-rich urban centre of brewing in the UK, a happy experience that had nothing to do with me. It continues to grow. For London to have as many breweries per head, it would need to have over 4,000.

One of Britain's favourite cities, Bristol's appeal comes from a mix of local design influences that include Brunel's magnificent feats of civil engineering, Aardman Animations' Wallace & Gromit, its attractively revived waterfront and extensive street art, inspired by Banksy and others. It also enjoys a well-earned and enviable reputation for independent restaurants and food shops, with a centuries-old side line in rioting as evidenced in 2021 by the toppling of the controversial statue to local merchant Edward Colston, who made his fortune, as did many in the city, from slave trading.

BEER VENUES

This is the only English city featured in this book, so let me explain that the UK beer industry is unique for shackling its pubs and bars to property companies that have complex and profound links to the largest brewing companies, leading to few outlets being free to choose what beers they sell. We British, having an island empire mentality, think this is normal.

The idea for this book came from a column I was allowed to write over several years in Bristol's highly informative local CAMRA magazine *Pints West*. When trying to apply my cloud-level method of describing a local beer scene to its home city, I realised that this doesn't work, so instead I will describe a particular street, and a cultural phenomenon.

▶ KING STREET

In a distinctly un-British example of city planning, most of central Bristol's more interesting beer bars are laced either side of the Old Vic Theatre, on King Street, an old, cobbled lane that parallels the Georgian splendour that is Queen Square. I first visited it as a student over 40 years ago, when it was renowned for its choice of cask ales, which sometimes reached nine at the weekend. It's changed a bit since then.

Starting at its western end, **Small Bar** (smallbar.co.uk) is an attractive, much stripped back and wooded two-storey gaff, serving dozens of beers from many countries and traditions, its cask ales served via minimalist handpulls, and its kitchen focused on burgers and chicken wings; on the opposite side of the street the cavernous **Famous Royal Naval Volunteer** (navyvolunteer.co.uk) leans more towards draught ales, modern pub grub, traditional Sunday lunch and massive shared plates, while the vaulted **Beer Emporium** (thebeeremporium.net) shop and cellar bar changes its beer offer like it's a hairstyle, though it sticks with pizza.

On the other side of Queen Charlotte Street, the nicely refurbished, imposing 17th-century **Llandoger Trow** (llandogertrow.co.uk) would pass for a large village inn but for the rare international beers that appear among its 32 taps, while the **King Street Brewhouse** (kingstreetbrewhouse.co.uk) barely gets a look-in for its home-brewed cask ales.

This rapid run-through omits two traditional pubs, a music and gaming venue with craft beers, and a cider bar across the way at the end, added for good measure. In all, King Street's bars sell well over 300 different beers in as many metres, and most are good.

▶ THE BRISTOL TAPHOUSES

Bristol's other great draw for the beer tourist is its plethora of breweries with front-of-house taprooms. Pre-COVID the norm was that these mainly opened at the weekend, from April to October. Then lockdown introduced many more Bristolians to their local brewers, fuelling moves to offer this year-round and on through the week.

Beyond King Street (above), Bristol's regular brewpubs are the huge, waterside **Left Handed Giant** (lhgbrewpub.com), tank beer specialists **ZeroDegrees** (zerodegrees.co.uk) opposite the Royal Infirmary, pub brews **Brewhouse & Kitchen** (brewhouseandkitchen.com) by Clifton Down station, and snuck under the railway arches at the back of Temple Meads station, **Little Martha** (littlemarthabrewing.co.uk).

Five minutes' walk beyond Little Martha is the pioneering bar at **Moor Beer** (moorbeer.co.uk), the first established year-round taproom, more recently joined by **BBF Tap** (bristolbeerfactory.co.uk) out

SMALL BAR

TABACCO FACTORY

NEED TO KNOW

The local CAMRA beer festival is in March and tends to be cask only, while the Craft Beer event on the quay is in August, featuring brewers' tents and music.

Accommodation: It makes sense to stay in the centre, within an easy walk of Temple Meads station transport, or if you prefer leafy historical, in Clifton, accessed from Temple Meads by taxi or the No. 8 bus. Between April and October there are big events on most weekends, the cost of lodgings varying with what those are.

Getting around: This is England, so public transport is pretty disjointed. There are many buses and a few urban train lines but no trams or metro. The only travelcards cost £6 for one day. Taxi ranks are rare and Uber is cheaper, except at busy times. The coolest transport is the waterbus that runs from the back of the station via the Arnolfini gallery and *SS Great Britain* to just short of Brunel's swing bridge.

Food: Bristol overflows with restaurants, including three with Michelin stars and examples of excellent cooking in most styles. There is no restaurant area as such and despite the choice, everywhere needs reserving on Friday and Saturday nights.

Hints: Other areas worth exploring for better beer pubs include Gloucester Road, said to be the longest street of independent shops left in the UK, and North Street as it winds through Bedminster to the Tobacco Factory and the Bristol Beer Factory (above).

at Southville, and **Fierce & Noble** (fierceandnoble.com) in St Werburgh's, whose near neighbours **Wiper & True** (wiperandtrue.com) may expand their hours from year-round weekends to include some weekdays when they complete a move to much larger premises in Old Market.

Other weekend taprooms include **Dawkins** (dawkinsgeorges.selz.com) in Easton and **Tapestry** (tapestrybrewery.com) in Totterdown, which is on the way from Temple Meads to Brislington, home of Bristol's most ambitious new brewer, **Lost & Grounded** (lostandgrounded.co.uk). Heading in the opposite direction and not far from Moor Beer in St Philips is **Good Chemistry** (goodchemistrybrewing.co.uk), from which you can walk on to the **New Bristol** (newbristolbrewery.co.uk) taproom, brewery and brewing school in St Paul's, and newcomer **Basement** (basementbeer.co.uk) in Stokes Croft.

Far from the scene becoming overcrowded, brewery crawling has become quite the thing in Bristol and business is on the rise. When Great Western brewery completes its relocation from the suburbs to become Hop Union in Brislington, a taproom will open, and with five other breweries not currently operating one, plus two more expected shortly, the range is set to get ever broader.

BRISTOL 73

ABOUT BRUSSELS

Population: City 1,019,000; metropolitan area 2,065,000

Local breweries: Cantillon (heritage), de la Senne, Ermitage, En Stoemelings, No Science, Beer Project (craft) and others.

Trains: Many regular trains stop at all three of central Brussels' main stations, North, Central and South (Midi), all of which connect with Antwerp (±45 per day; 0.7-1 hour); and Luxembourg (±5 a day; 3.3 hours), while most high-speed trains use only Midi, which has direct connections with Amsterdam (±22 a day; 1.75-2.75 hours), and Paris (±14 a day; 1.4 hours) and one-change connections to Hamburg and Berlin. Eurostar also runs direct trains between Midi and London St Pancras (1.9-2.3 hours).

Airport: Brussels Zaventem airport is 12km NE of the city and has direct flights to/from many UK regional airports and the rest of Europe. Six trains an hour take 20-25 minutes to/from the centre (€9 each way). Taxis are roughly €50 to/from the centre. Don't even consider the bus. 'Brussels South' airport is near Charleroi, 1.5 hours away, with no direct train.

Currency: Euro (€)

BRUSSELS

Most of the institutions that decide what the brewing industry and everyone else in Europe should and should not do are based in Brussels. This is why its resident population swells by over 20% between Monday morning and Friday afternoon, which in turn accounts for why this is a city best visited at the weekend.

Despite Belgium's awesome reputation for making 'artisanal' beers, the best of which are found bottled with live yeast, the politicos here always used to drink wine, while the locals necked glasses of Jupiler, Maes, Stella or some other dull industrial lager. I say 'used to' because the past decade has seen a remarkable transition in tastes that has led the way for the creation of half a dozen new, city-based brewers, a rise in the demand for most of the traditional forms of Lambic beers – in traditional form a unique specialty of this region – and a dramatic shift away from industrial brands to those from small independent breweries old and new, albeit mostly still Belgian.

Brussels' only must-see tourist sight is its impossibly ornate Grand Place, the visual impact of which is stunning if you enter via one of its side alleys. The key to enjoying the Manneken Pis is to watch the crowd snapping it; the early morning junkfest on Place du Jeu de Balle is for spotting pearls among the trinkets; the space-age Atomium symbolises the dream of a more positive era; and the Magritte Museum is Belgianism on canvas.

BEER VENUES

The doyens of the new Brussels beer world, Brasserie de la Senne, sell a lot of obviously excellent beer in Brussels and have set a high standard for other local brewers. In contrast, do not attempt to drink Lambic beers without studying the style first. The best names in Lambic are the city's own Cantillon brewery, and from neighbouring Payottenland Boon, Tilquin, Oud Beersel, Drie Fonteinen (3F), De Cam, Girardin and newcomers Lambiek Fabriek.

➤ POECHENELLEKELDER

🛈 5 Rue du Chêne – poechenellekelder.be – *shut Mo; Fr-Sa 11.00-02.00; others 11.00-01.00*

The Poech is bang opposite the Manneken Pis, and its terrace is the ideal place for watching the crowd trying to make sense of the world's most famous pot-bellied, widdling midget. Home to an occasional puppet theatre in its basement and some great bric-a-brac in its main bar, the pick of 130 Belgian beers is one of the best in Belgium.

BRUSSELS 75

► MOEDER LAMBIC FONTAINAS

🛈🍴 8 Place Fontainas – moederlambic.com – *Sa-Su 14.00-24.00; Mo-Fr 16.00-24.00 – tram 3, 4 & 32: Anneessens*

Sit at a high stool on the long bar, at an orderly table or out on the less orderly terrace to sample from one of the most interesting selections of draught beers in Europe, often featuring a 'country of the week', and at least one draught Lambic. There are unusual bottles too, many in 75cl sharers. Food is advanced cheese plates and other snacks.

► BROCANTE

🛈🍴 170 Rue Blaes – FB/cafelabrocante – *daily from before breakfast to mid-evening*

On the corner of the Jeu de Balle flea market is this traditional street corner boozer with an exceptional menu of Lambic beers, a decent list of ales, a basic bar menu, live lunchtime music at weekends, a small tree-lined terrace and bizarre opening hours dictated by customers who buy and sell on the square.

MONK

CANTILLON

▶ LES BRIGITTINES
🍴 Place de la Chapelle 5 – lesbrigittines.com – *shut Mo; others 12.00-15.00 & 18.00-22.00*

You don't just roll up here for a beer. You make a booking, spruce yourself, add smart casual, or white tie if you prefer, and sit down to conversation over your best meal of the trip. At the city end of the antiques and curios of Rue Blaes, it oozes unforced class and cultured ambience, the cuisine complemented by a short but elite list of greats.

▶ DELIRIUM VILLAGE
🛈 Impasse de la Fidélité – deliriumvillage.com – *daily 10.00-06.00 – metro: De Brouckère*

Four beer cafés and a couple of spirits bars work as one in this alleyway off Rue des Bouchers, home to the #MeToo Jeanneken-Pis, in the Îlot Sacré restaurant enclave. The Delirium Café cellar stocks over 2,000 beers, the Monasterium sells abbey beers and vodka, Hoppy Loft does IPAs et al, and the Taphouse has 27 taps. No food.

▶ BRASSINS
🛈 Keyenveld 36 – lesbrassins.be – *Sa-Su 13.00-01.00; others 12.00-15.00 & 18.00-23.00 – tram 8, 92, 93 & 97: Stéphanie*

Just outside the Brussels Ring, a 10-minute walk from Porte de Namur and Louise metro stations, is this archetypal Bruxellois bistro with beer. You won't find a more typical menu – try the rabbit in Kriek or ham-wrapped chicory in cheese sauce. There is a good selection of 75cl sharer bottles among its 60 beers. Audrey Hepburn was born nearby.

▶ MONK
🛈🍴 Rue Sainte Catherine 42 – monk.be – *Su 13.00-01.00; Fr-Sa 11.00-03.00; others 11.00-01.00 – metro: De Brouckère*

Named for jazz pianist Thelonious rather than any Trappist brewer, this 80-beer Art Deco bar and spaghetti bolognaise dispensary has evolved nicely over the years. It is the source of the rumour that spag bol is a Bruxellois invention. Also, its gentlemen's urinal is the only place from which to view the underside of the city's old town wall.

▶ GIST

🛈 Place de la Vieille Halle aux Blés 30 – gistbeerandco.business.site – *shut Su-Mo; others 16.00-01.00 – central area*

Turn right on leaving the Poech to reach the square with this stark but classy bar and its small terrace. It took Brussels a while to catch on to the modern take on craft beer, being the capital city of the country that inspired it. Here is where the ancient and modern blend, in draught and bottled. Nibbles only but several restaurants nearby.

The other trail worth considering is twinning some brewery visits. To the southwest of the Ring, the unique and strangely beautiful **Cantillon Lambic brewery** (cantillon.be; shut We & Su; others 10.00-16.00) is the most visited in Belgium, and now has the **Ermitage** ale brewery nearby (ermitagenanobrasserie.be; Fr-Sa 14.00-22.00), while to its northwest, at the other end of the city, the taproom at de La Senne's impressive new brewhouse near the Flemish civil service building has pop-up food, and possible side trips to the more basic digs of **En Stoemelings** (enstoemelings.be) and **No Science** (Fr 13.00-17.00), both in nearby Rue Dieudonné Lefèvre.

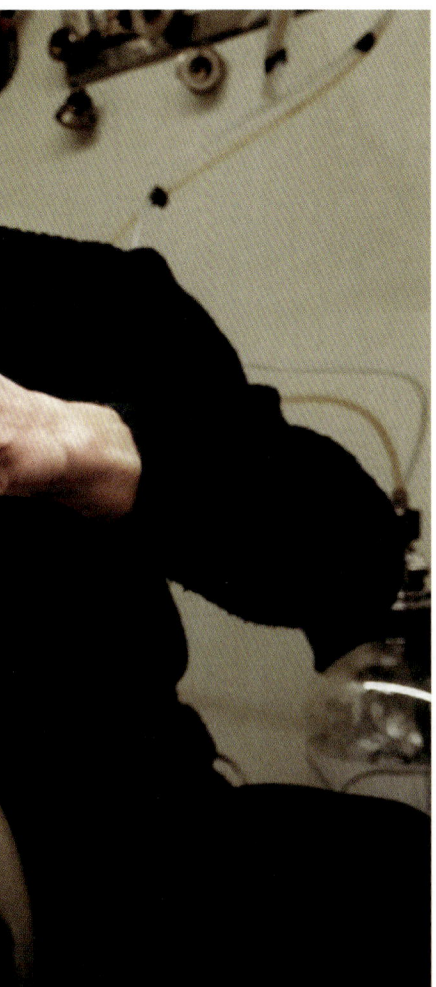

GIST

NEED TO KNOW

From Brussels, most places in Belgium are an easy day trip. The country is a treasure trove of dotty local traditions, bizarre museums and quaint, often edgy local festivals. Brussels has also been the crossroads of Europe since long before the EU arrived. Be prepared to hear four different languages in a single sentence, plus a distinctive patois reserved for the locals.

Accommodation: Expect wild variations in prices depending on whether or not the European Parliament is in session, or there is a major event. The area around Place Ste Catherine makes a great base, for being central, well connected, and a decent neighbourhood, all in one. Try vintagehotel.be and zoomhotel.be, near Place Louise, for great beer lists.

Getting around: The central area is being pedestrianised by stealth. For elsewhere the public transport system is complex but fully integrated, with tickets valid on the metro, tram, bus and local train systems, though tickets are no longer available on board so all journeys must be bought by bank card or for regulars a Mobib travel card. The trips cost €2.10 each up to a maximum of €7.50 for 24 hours.

Food: For local nibbles try tête pressée or kip-kap, or hope to encounter obscure cheeses and variants on cooked sausage. For the staples choose a piece of meat with frites and a sauce. For an eye-opening culinary delight choose something unpronounceable that makes only partial sense in English. Be daring, fear nothing, you only live once – Brussels does great food.

Hints: Tipping involves rounding up only. CAMRA Books' *Good Beer Guide Belgium* is a legendary and unsurpassed resource.

ABOUT BUDAPEST

- **Population:** 1,775,000
- **Local breweries:** Balkezes, Fehér Nyúl, Horizont, HopTop, Legenda, Mad Scientist, Monyo and others (craft).
- **Trains:** Budapest-Keleti station, just off the central area, has its own metro station and direct connections with Vienna (±12 a day; 2.6 hours); and Prague (±6 a day; 7.1-7.6 hours).
- **Airport:** Budapest Ferenc Liszt airport is 20km SE of the centre and has direct connections with Heathrow, Gatwick, Stansted, Luton and seven regional UK airports. The 100E bus runs between the airport and Kálvin, Astoria and Deák Ferenc metro stations and costs HUF900 each way. The 200E runs from Terminal 2 to Ferihegy train station, with ±100 daily connections with the centre, then Kőbanya-Kispest metro. The BKK app explains well. Official Főtaxis should cost HUF7000-9000 each way.
- **Currency:** Hungarian Forint (HUF) 419 = £ 1 (Feb 2022)

BUDAPEST

The Hungarian capital straddles the Danube, the riverfront showcasing architecture from the height of the Austro-Hungarian Empire to make it one of the most striking cities in the world.

Historically Hungarians display equal preferences for drinking beer, wine and spirits. The country's beer scene is both young and old. One of the all-time brewing greats, Anton Dreher, opened a fully formed lager brewery in the city in the 1880s, bringing large-scale beer production to a country previously content with sweet wines from Tokay and robust reds like Bulls Blood, or else knocking back adventurous spirits such as Unicum, one of the world's most extraordinary drinks.

In modern terms craft brewing started here late, though it is catching up rapidly. There are no indigenous Hungarian beer styles as such, and the scene is influenced equally by older Czech and modern American preferences. The same could be said of its pubs.

Budapest feels more 'foreign' than much of Europe, which can feed a desire to explore it more than elsewhere. The Danube must be cruised, the castle and its catacombs explored, and the waters of the Széchenyi Medicinal Baths taken. But try to make a couple of other visits, to the museum of pinball machines or retro design, or of spirits miniatures at Zwack Unicum.

BEER VENUES

The Hungarian language is impenetrable, so research your destinations in advance, and plot their relationship to the well-designed public transport network. The city now has over 100 bars with a good range of beers, these dividing into distinct sub-types that I have tried to illustrate below.

▶ CSAK A JÓ SŐR (ONLY GOOD BEER)

🍺🍴 Kertész utca 42 – csakajosor.hu
– shut Su; Mo-Sa 14.00-22.00 – tram 4, 6: Király utca, trolley 70, 78: Erzsébet körút

One of the best stocked beer shops in Europe helped to change modern Hungary's attitude to beer by its efforts to import the very best and to promote local start-ups. First and foremost a shop with six taps and a great selection of 200+ beers from around the world, it transforms by evening into a chatty tasting room frequented by all sorts.

▶ ÉLESZTŐHÁZ

🍺🍴 Tűzoltó útca 22 – elesztohaz.hu
– daily from 15.00 – metro 3: Corvyn-negyed

If Budapest has a bar style all its own, it is the ruin bar, typically laced round the insides of a disused factory or warehouse, with distressed furnishings and all manner

HUNGARIAN BEERS FROM HEDDON

of junk on the walls, creating a slovenly heap with enough space to feel comfortable. 'The Yeast House' is my favourite, for its eclectic top-rate beer range and extensive bar food.

▶ HOPAHOLIC

🛈 Akácfa utca 38 - hopaholic.hu – *shut Su; Mo-We 16.00-24.00; Th-Sa 16.00-02.00 - metro M2: Blaha Lujza*

Quieter than some and just out of the centre, this smallish two-level beer bar and cellar was Budapest's first unashamedly craft beer-focused pub. Its dozen taps come from all over Europe, though the bottle and can list typically runs to about 50 Hungarian beers in a list nearing 200. Small snacks are available to tide you over.

▶ KEG SÖRMŰVHÁZ

🛈 🍴 Orlay utca 1 - kegsormuvhaz.hu – *Th-Sa 12.00-24.00; Su-Tu 12.00-23.00 - metro M4, trams 19, 41, 47, 48. 49, 56: Szent Gellért*

The smart, family friendly Keg bistro, in a cask cellar on the Buda side of town not far from Szabadság bridge, operates to a simple model. Its list of just over 30 beers – all on tap – has more than 50% from newer Hungarian brewers, while the burger menu is bolstered by beef stroganoff, and duck breast, suggesting it as a lunch or dinner venue.

▶ HETEDIK LÉPSCSŐ

🛈 🍴 Rákóczi út 13 - FB/hetedillepcso – *shut Su-Mo; Tu-Sa from 14.00 - metro M2, trams 47, 48. 49, trolley 72: Astoria*

The Czech influence on the Budapest beer

scene reached a new level with this airy modern bar specialising in the Czech take on craft beer and food. Owned by the same people as the more traditionally Bohemian Hrabal (hrabalsorozo.hu – daily from 14.00), a couple of doors down, where both beer and food are more solid heritage stuff.

▸ BELGIAN BRASSERIE HENRI

🍽 **Bem Rakpart 12 – belgasorozo.com** – daily 12.00-24.00 – tram 19, 41: Halász utca

Flying the flag for Belgian ales on the Buda bank of the city for 25 years, the well-worn path trodden by its solid list of 80+ beers and efforts at Flemish-Hungarian cooking, shared with its nearby cousin Pater Marcus (patermarcus.hu – Apor Péter utca 1 – daily 12.00-24.00) may need refreshing but has undoubtedly influenced beer here.

NEED TO KNOW

Like much of Central Europe, Budapest gets hellish cold in winter and just as hot in summer. Formed by the fusion of more leisurely Buda, on the castle side of the river, with Pest on the city centre side, the Hungarian capital has seven bridges of which the Széchenyi Chain Bridge is the most famous.

🛏 **Accommodation:** There are the usual seasonal variations in price, though expect lower than average for Europe. A few of the hotels on the Buda side have river level exits at the front and rooftop level exits to the castle at the back. Affordable grandeur is available at times.

🚇 **Getting around:** Walking is a good option for much of the centre. Public transport is run by BKK (bkk.hu), and tickets cover the metro, trams, trolleys, most buses and local trains, and on weekdays on some Danube ferries. Get the app or buy a travelcard from a purple machine for 10 journeys (HUF3000), 24 hours (HUF1650), 72 hours (HUF4150) or 7 days (HUF4950). A 24-hour card for up to 5 people costs HUF4550.

🍴 **Food:** The focus on goulasch is over-stated, though excellent examples abound. Roast goose is the real speciality. Mediterranean influence is everywhere, central European staples in pork and cabbage gain paprika and other spices, supplemented by pepper-tomato-aubergine-courgette concoctions. Smoked freshwater fish is an acquired taste.

⭐ **Hints:** Tipping at 10% is standard for bars, restaurants and taxis. Do not expect the green light on a pedestrian crossing to offer protection.

ABOUT COPENHAGEN

Population: City 640,000; metropolitan area 1,370,000

Local breweries: Carlsberg (global); Amager, Mikkeller Baghaven & To Øl (craft); Nørrebro & Warpigs (brewpub), among others.

Trains: Elegant København H (Hovedbanegård), has direct connections with Stockholm (±6 a day; 5.2-6 hours); and Hamburg (±4 a day; 4.5-5 hours).

Airport: Copenhagen Kastrup airport is 9km from the city centre and has direct connections with Heathrow, Gatwick, Stansted and Luton, plus five regional airports. Driverless metro trains run every 5 minutes or so between Terminal 3 and Vanløse taking 15 minutes to/from centrally located Nørreport station. An S-train connects every 10 minutes with København H. All are covered by the City Pass (see Need to know). Taxis are expensive and slower.

Ferry port: Ferries sail between Copenhagen and Oslo daily (17 hours), from just beyond the Little Mermaid statuette.

Currency: Danish Krone (DKK) 8.80 ±0.5 = £1 (Feb 2022)

COPENHAGEN

Don't tell the Canadians but the most contented country in the world is Denmark. Partly it is to do with the hygge – an untranslatable word intended to epitomise an inner cosiness that comes from embracing the simpler things in life.

Copenhagen is the home of industrial brewing's most ethical giant, Carlsberg, green in more than label and originator of more scientific advances in brewing than Pasteur and monasticism combined. Its other superstar is beer design guru Mikkel Bjergsø, as in Mikkeller, whose mostly Belgian- and US-brewed boutique beers and chi-chi bars sprinkle magic dust on parts of the old inner city.

Beyond these contrasting giants lies a rich seam of reliable new breweries producing a better class of new-style IPAs and a wealth of seriously interesting Porters and Stouts, not least a chart-topping range of Imperial ones. As well as the locals, check the list for Bad Luck, Crooked Stave, Dry & Bitter, Hornbeer, or, if you are lucky, Ebeltoft.

For major tourism, the Tivoli gardens still has its fans, though the Nyhavn waterfront entertainment area may be more to your taste. The iconic statue of the Little Mermaid is almost as tiny as the portions served in the more expensive restaurants.

BEER VENUES

To hone down your sampling of Danish beer, look for the Scandinavian talent for huge grain, add the smooth and reliable traditions from south of the Baltic, and spice it with some craft extremism. Quietly understated Copenhagen hosts a highly accomplished beer scene, akin to the intense detail of TV dramas like *Borgen* or *The Bridge*. From over 100 possible recommendations these are the top examples.

▶ PEDERS

🛈 Sankt Peders Stræde 31 – pederscph.dk – *Fr-Sa 14.00-02.00; Su-Th 14.00-24.00 – metro M3, M4: Rådhuspladsen*

Traditionally low down the tickers' lists of the city's famous beer bars but for me the

coolest. A seriously stylish, downmarket cellar bar not far from Ørsted Park, with a list of up to 200 beers, including perhaps the best Danish selection in town, epitomising the new Danish beer scene. Food is limited to nuts, wasabi peas and the occasional cake.

▶ FERMENTORUM

🛈 Halmtorvet 29C – fermentorum.com – *Mo-We from 15.00; Th-Su from 14.00 – S-train A, B, C, E, H: Dybbølsbro*

My worst hangover of all time followed an evening when beer world glitterati kept arriving at this excellent ale bar each time I tried to leave – if only it had served some food. Forgive the crowded house vibe and concentrate on the candlelight, finding time to applaud the imaginative and ever-changing tap and bottle lists. Not far from Warpigs.

▶ ØRESTED ØLBAR

🛈 Norre Farimagsgade 13 – FB/ Ørsted-Ølbar – *Tu-Fr from 15.00; Sa from 13.00, Su 14.00, Mo from 16.00 – metro M1, M2: Nørreport*

I love the lived-in feel of this evergreen, candlelit, cellar-level drinking place, by the side of Ørsted Park. One of the city's longest serving beer bars, it usually stocks Denmark's original craft beer, Limfjords Porter (7.9%). Another long-established haunt is Himmeriget (Åboulevard 27 – FB/ himmeriget – shut Mo; Tu-Su from 16.00), on the other side of the canal.

▶ TAPHOUSE

🛈 Lavendelstræde 15 – taphouse.dk – *Mo-Th 15.00-02.00; Fr-Sa 12.00-03.00; Su 12.00-24.00 – metro M3, M4: Rådhuspladsen*

Slap-bang in the centre, with over 60 beers on tap. Classic styles come from Germany, the Czech Republic, Belgium, Scandinavia and elsewhere to bolster the wilder craft offerings, while food stops at sausage. Its first manager went on to broaden the concept to include bottles, cans and food at Skaal (Kultorvet 11 – skaal.dk – daily from 11.30).

▶ BARR

🛈 Strandgade 93 – restaurantbarr.com – *shut Mo-Tu; We-Th 17.00-23.00; Fr-Su 12.00-23.00 – metro M1, M2, M3, M4: Kongens Nytorv*

Across the Inderhavns bridge from Nyhavn, this used to be the site of Europe's most expensive restaurant, Noma. Book to dine in style at the new place, at a price, or drop in to its thoughtfully concocted, all-wooden beer bar to take beer with masterful nibbles, superbly but expensively. You don't come here on a pub crawl.

BAGHAVEN

TAPHOUSE

▶ BAGHAVEN

🛈 🍴 **Refshalevej 169b – mikkeller.com**
– Mo-Th from 14.00; Fr from 13.00; Sa-Su from 12.00 – Bus 2A Refshaleøen

Mikkeller was fledged in Copenhagen, where it has returned to roost. Famed for creating outlandish beers, most clever and some exceedingly good, its finest creation to date is this barrel-ageing warehouse with bar and sustenance, on a wharf reached by bus from København H station. Drink the unthinkable or think it undrinkable, you will remember it. Their eleven other beer businesses in town are also good.

NEED TO KNOW

It would not be unusual to return from a trip to Copenhagen and, when asked what you did, say 'Well nothing really'. How such a grey place, with so few memorable sights, brings out a glow is all part of its secret.

🛏 **Accommodation:** Hotels are expensive but often discount deeply for bookings made well in advance. Standards are generally high. Aim for the centre or anywhere a simple ride from København H.

🚇 **Getting around:** A 'small' City Pass gets you onto all metro, train and bus services in the city, and for the airport. Buy one at most transport hubs or 7/11 kiosks for DKK80-300, covering 24 to 120 hours. The Copenhagen Card adds free admissions to 80 attractions.

🍴 **Food:** To avoid feeding the burger-pizza-BBQ monster try smørrebrød, open rye bread sandwiches topped with leverpostej (liver paste), shrimp & egg, red beef & gherkin, shrimp & roe, or others. Thick cuts of smoked or cured salmon play well too, as does mørbradøffer (chunky pork tenderloin in rich sauce).

⭐ **Hints:** Tipping is not essential. Jaywalking is fined. Most people speak English. Being drunk is pitied.

SKAAL

COPENHAGEN

ABOUT DUBLIN

- **Population:** City 1,430,000
- **Local breweries:** Guinness (heritage); Porterhouse, Lineman, Whiplash, Stone Barrel and others (craft).
- **Trains:** The city's two main stations, Heuston, W of the centre and S of the river, and Connolly, E of the centre and N of the river provide between them direct connections to most places on the Irish network, to all of the country's ferry ports but not the airport.
- **Airport:** Dublin Airport is 10km N of the centre and has direct flights to/from over 100 cities in Europe, including a dozen in the UK, plus four in North America. Kavanagh's Airport bus takes 20 minutes and costs €9 each way, while regular bus routes 16 and 41 take 40-50 minutes and cost €3.50. Taxis go from Terminal 1 and cost roughly €30 each way.
- **Ferry port:** Dublin port is two miles to the E of the city centre and has direct ferries to/from Liverpool (8 hours, up to 3 a day), Holyhead (3.2-3.5 hours, up to 6 a day) and Cherbourg (France – 18-19 hours, up to 3 a week)
- **Currency:** Euro (€)

DUBLIN

Ireland's capital is bisected by the River Liffey as it flows to the city's port. Famed too much for revelry, it is every bit as much a sober place. Its new status as the largest English-speaking city in the EU has added to many subtle influences that in combination over the past four decades have seen it become greatly more self-respecting.

Until the mid-1990s the Irish brewing scene was entirely dominated by three breweries – Dutch Heineken, British Bass and Irish Guinness. Today, replace Bass with the brand brokerage C&C, owners of Magners cider and other concoctions, and the picture is largely the same, but for an increasingly confident and growing clutch of small breweries that make an abundance of brews in heritage and newer styles.

Ireland is a nation far more influenced by the US than the UK, though at its best when its inimitable self. Irish drinkers and craft brewers adopted tropical hops with gusto a few years back, though nowadays, perhaps inevitably, it is coming to be Porters and Stouts that are more expected of them.

The city at its country's head endures a not entirely unearned reputation for drinking itself to incoherence for the least excuse, but don't be misled by this. Drinking beer in Dublin today is a far more sophisticated experience.

BEER VENUES

Like all the best beer-related traditions, the great Irish pub is largely a confection, designed in this case so that the larger players in the Irish brewing industry can keep control of the on-trade. When small beer began to fight back in the mid 1990s, its inroads into the pub scene were kept at bay by loan arrangements and tap purchases made by the large suppliers. The love of music and banter, and the people who join in with this, are the only authentic parts.

▶ PORTERHOUSE TEMPLE BAR
🛈 🍴 16-18 Parliament Street – porterhousebrewco.ie – *daily from 14.00*

Entering Temple Bar from Grattan Bridge, pay homage to the pub that started Ireland's slow return from plaything of three large brewery companies to a resolute creator of great small breweries. Enjoy a huge range of global beers, many Irish, a dozen from the Porterhouse brewery and several must-try Stouts. Live music every evening. Pub grub enough to sustain. For more space and mahogany, try Porterhouse Central (47 Nassau Street – Mo-Th 14.00-23.30; Fr-Su 12.30-23.30).

▶ UNDERDOG

🛈 **75 Dame Street - FB/UnderDog-Dublin-812139445602353** – *Sa-Su from 15.00; Mo-Fr from 17.00*

Just up from City Hall, snuck underneath the more ostentatious Brogan's Bar, within the Temple Bar entertainment district, is this much-loved, well-stocked cellar bar, founded by two well-known figures in the craft brewing world. No food but a good vibe and great staff, plus one of the best thought-through, ever-changing beer lists in the country.

▶ P. MACS

🛈 🍴 **30 Stephen Street Lower – FB/pmacspub** – *Fr-Sa 12.00-01.00; Su-Th 12.00-24.00*

A few doors down from Craft Central (below), on the way from Temple Bar to Stephens Green park and shopping centre, this was the city's first seriously accomplished craft beer bar, bringing a welcome combination of a wide range of international craft beers, a warm atmosphere with candles and alcoves, clever food and knowledgeable staff.

▶ CRAFT CENTRAL (STEPHEN STREET NEWS)

🛒 **38 Stephen Street Lower – craftcentral.ie** – *Th-Sa 10.30-22.00; Mo-We 10.30-21.00; Su 12.20-21.30*

Before COVID the still excellent Drink Store

(87 Manor Street – drinkstore.ie), just up the way from L Mulligan Grocer (below) was Dublin's top beer shop. With lockdown, this hardworking specialist provider has outgrown the newsagent shop that hosts it, to offer 300+ mostly canned beers from the craft end of Irish, British and US brewing,

PORTERHOUSE TEMPLE BAR

UNDERDOG

NEED TO KNOW

Read up a bit on Irish history from the Irish perspective, if only to avoid the more irritating forms of ignorance. With 2021 being the 100th anniversary of Irish independence from Britain, much has been forgiven, though Brexit has not helped. If in doubt, welcome clarification, question nothing and turn the talk to Stout.

🛏 **Accommodation:** Dublin's rising stock in Europe has led to a basic choice of higher priced central accommodation, which can be noisy, or staying in a quieter, leafier area close to one of the tram routes.

🚊 **Getting around:** The centre is mostly walkable. An integrated suburban train and tram system run by TFI (transportforireland.ie) is mostly for out-of-centre trips. Bus routes are plentiful but designed for locals. A TFI Leap Card brings discounts, bought online and topped up through an app. 30-minute trips <3 km cost €1.60; 90-minutes €2.30. 24-hour and 7-day ticket prices depend on which zones are covered. Uber and Bolt operate everywhere.

🍴 **Food:** The old national staple, potato, is best when creamed with spring onion as champ, or with cabbage as colcannon. The alternative national carb is soda bread, leavened with bicarb and buttermilk. Dublin Bay prawns are a type of langoustine, or scampi. The most typical local sausage is white pudding, like black but without the blood.

⭐ **Hints:** For insider knowledge about breweries, beers and outlets, visit beoir.org, the website of Ireland's beer consumer group Beoir, which is also cheap and easy to support by joining.

▶ L MULLIGAN GROCER

ℹ 🍴 18 Stoneybatter – lmulligangrocer.com – *Mo-Th 16.00-23.30; Fr 16.00-00.30; Sa 12.30-00.30; Su 12.30-23.00 – Red tram: Smithfield*

There are those who consider this old-fashioned Dublin bar and eatery a bit tatty but they have no sense of style. Looks should not be a big thing when the beer list has supported small Irish brewers for decades and that within its bottled menu of 100+ has a self-proclaimed 'RidicuList' of rare and expensive beers from far and near. Excellent veggie and other variants on pub staples too.

▶ 57 THE HEADLINE BAR

ℹ 🍴 56-57 Clanbrassil Street Lower – *57theheadline.com – shut Mo; Su from 13.00; Tu-Sa from 16.00*

Just off the South Circular Road, beyond the visitable Teeling Whiskey Distillery, the foodiest of our entries has nonetheless a wide range of beers, including a strong offering of draught and canned beers from smaller Irish brewers. Badly rocked by COVID but unbowed, its normal shtick also includes numerous events, including beer talks.

ABOUT EDINBURGH

Population: 520,000

Local breweries: Heineken Caledonian (heritage); Campervan, Newbarns, Pilot, Stewart and quite a few others (craft).

Trains: Centrally located Waverley station has direct connections with much of Scotland, and southwards into England, including a direct line to Bristol (±10 a day; 6.5 hours).

Airport: Edinburgh airport is 8 miles W of the city, with direct connections with all London airports including City, Bristol, six other regional airports and much of the rest of Europe. Given the trouble it took, it would be rude not to use the frequent tram service, which takes 20-30 minutes to/from the centre and costs £6.50 single, £9 return. Buses are a bit cheaper and slower. Taxis cost £25-30 each way.

Currency: British Pound (£)

EDINBURGH

The Scottish seat of government is not one city, but two; the first opens, freshly swept, in early September, then disappears into a maze of scaffolding in July, in readiness for the Edinburgh Festival, the largest cultural event on the planet, which takes over the entire city every August.

When England objected to losing cask ale in the 1970s, Scotland was already well into a lager revolution, with brands like Tennent's considered a cut above the soft, sweet, light-brown kegged ales that were the common alternative.

It took considerable campaigning effort to preserve and revive the cask ale tradition in Scotland, but half a century later local beer lovers have the twin challenges of how to absorb an older tradition of 'Scotch' ales, while eclectic craft brewers pop up at random. The UK's most prestigious brewing school, Herriot Watt, is based here, its alumni influencing the scene, not least the creators of the UK's most successful new brewery in over a century, Scottish wunderkind BrewDog.

BEER VENUES

The Edinburgh pub scene is one of the best in Britain, with classics such as neighbours the Guildford Arms and Café Royal (West Register Street), Bennet's Bar (8 Leven Street), Inspector Rebus's Oxford Bar (8 Young Street) and the superb Leslie's Bar (45 Ratcliffe Terrace, Mayfield), failing to make full listings for underplaying non-cask beers.

▶ THE HANGING BAT

🛈 🍴 133 Lothian Road – thehangingbat.com – Mo-Sa 12.00-01.00; Su 12.30-01.00 – bus 11, 16, 24: Bread Street

It is fine to hate this place. They don't serve pints, the beer menu is as mainstream as any Classical play list, the house brews are rarely straight, and chatting quietly is as easy as in a blast furnace. However, in its time it has served to shake a load of dust off what was becoming quite a complacent beer scene. Hot dogs and ribs are seen as food.

▶ BOW BAR

🛈 🍴 80 West Bow – thebowbar.co.uk – daily 02.00 -24.00 – Grassmarket bus & coach station

Considerably less ancient than it appears but nonetheless a great chieftain o' the pubbing race, just uphill from Grassmarket in the Old Town. Note the uniquely Scottish tall founts used for the cask ales. Take these with fresh soup, pies or a great range of single malts. Along with its cousin, the Stockbridge Tap (2 Raeburn Place – daily 12.00-24.00), just beyond the New Town, a role model for any old-style pub wanting to keep pace with beerier times.

▶ CLOISTERS BAR

🛈🍴 26 Brougham Street – cloistersbar.com – *Mo-Th 12.00-24.00; Fr-Sa 12.00-01.00; Su 12.30-24.00 – bus 24: Brougham Street*

Like a pub only grander, perhaps for being a former parsonage. It is easy to while away time in its elegant, stone and dark wood rooms, which are agreeably short on music. Up to 20 pulls or taps and two dozen bottled ales emphasise breweries that are small, Scottish and independent. The food is broader and more accomplished than elsewhere.

▶ BRAUHAUS

🛈 105 Lauriston Place – linktr.ee/brauhaus – *Fr-Su 15.00-01.00; others 16.00-01.00 – bus 27, 35: Lauriston Place*

One of the UK's most eccentric elite pubs is easily left undiscovered or worse, found and passed by. The beer selection, like the 'natural' wines and whisky selection, is cleverly hand-picked. The furnishings, in contrast, look like they were rescued from a church hall's closing down sale. Expect studied service, an eclectic mix of beers in all styles and formats, no food and the occasional super-expensive rare malt.

▶ MONTY'S

🛈🍴 185 Morrison Street – montys.bar – *Su from 12.30; others from 12.00 – train, tram & bus: Haymarket Station*

This nice-looking beer and whisky bar is a first and last stop for Edinburgh's other train station, Haymarket. Downstairs is small, upstairs tiny. Up to a dozen draught beers include at least four in cask, with another fifty in bottle or can, chosen for breadth more than depth. Great cold platters. Thomson's Bar (daily 12.00-24.00), opposite, is a classic too.

▶ SALT HORSE BEER SHOP & BAR

🛈🍴 57-61 Blackfriars Street – salthorse.beer – *Shop: daily 14.00-21.00 daily; Bar: Mo-Tu 16.00-23.00; Fr-Sa 12.00-24.00; others 12.00-23.00 – bus 35: Museum of Childhood*

Primarily a shop with ±350 bottles and cans for take-home, focusing on Scottish and

up-market craft brews. A couple of doors up, its small bar has a courtyard at the rear and will, at quieter times, serve most of the stuff from the shop at a mark-up. There are also a dozen beers on tap. The bar snacks are far better than average too.

CAFE ROYAL

NEED TO KNOW

Between October and May learn the meaning of 'wind-chill factor', the thing that freezes your bones through your troosers. If you are going to the Festival, allow a week, plan your shows in advance, and expect crowds.

Accommodation: At Festival time look at University residences. For the rest of the year go for apartments in either the Old or New Town, or research carefully the many hundreds of B&Bs for location, bus links and local pubs (via whatpub.com).

Getting around: The tram is mostly for the airport, urban trains don't help much and although buses are plentiful, they are run by different companies that operate their own ticketing systems. Single fares cost £1.80 and a day ticket £4.50. Taxis are impressively efficient and relatively cheap for the UK.

Food: Scottish food comes in three layers. On top is superb, locally-sourced offerings from top notch chefs; in the middle are great traditional baking and comfort foods, including the much-gentrified haggis, tatties & neeps; while at the base is cardiotoxic filth, such as deep-fried pizza pie, or chocolate bars in soggy batter.

Hints: You can buy single malt whisky cheaper online. A better consumable souvenir is weapons grade haggis in a tin. For gory tourism avoid all dungeons and ghost tours and visit the medical museums instead.

EDINBURGH

GIBRALTAR

OK reader, it's time to drop your smug complacency. Decent beer did not start returning to the world on merit alone. Its re-emergence involved disgruntled beer drinkers persuading bar owners to stock better beers and give them a chance to shine. This is your job in Gibraltar, should you pick up the challenge.

For those who don't know it, 'The Rock' is a single, tight community descended from ex-pat Italian, Maltese, British and occasionally

ABOUT GIBRALTAR

- **Population:** 34,000
- **Local breweries:** None.
- **Trains:** The nearest station is Algeciras in neighbouring Spain, which has direct connections with Barcelona (2 a day; 17 hours). Most taxis stop at the border.
- **Airport:** Gibraltar's airport is squeezed onto the land between the Rock and the Spanish border and has direct connections with Heathrow, Gatwick, Bristol, Edinburgh and Manchester. By far the easiest option for most transfers is a taxi.
- **Currency:** British Pound (£)

BEER BREAKS

Spanish workers, traditionally dependent on a naval base that helped Britannia rule the waves, and a neat sideline in smuggling, mostly of cigarettes.

As UK defence spending dropped, this fiercely loyal, English-speaking 'overseas territory' needed a new economic base and so adopted a role as a financial centre – like the Isle of Man or Channel Isles but with more sun – attracting those who dislike paying their intended share of tax.

More recently a new, younger population of 'anywhere-but-Britain' trainee ex-pats have come to this mini-world, hemmed into 6.7 square miles of infertile peninsula, draped around a striking rocky outcrop. This odd melee of rich-but-tight, poor-but-optimistic and worried-but-loyal populations makes for great people watching, in a unique place with loads of weather.

The Rock itself is best ascended by cable car, then descended via its amazing tunnels, and winding footpaths patrolled by macaques, also known as Barbary apes, the cute thugs that snatch headwear and unzip bags, targeting spectacles, keys and jewellery.

BEER VENUES

The problem with trying to brew here is that most water comes from a desalination plant, as the short-lived Gib Gun brewery discovered to its cost in 2018. The nearest thing to a local ale is Barbary Beer (4.4%), a bottled brew commissioned from Bushy's on the tax-averse Isle of Man, which features hops grown in Gib's Botanical Gardens and has the character of a northern Best Bitter.

The colony has been gagging for a more sophisticated night economy for decades and bits are starting to emerge. Traditionally awash with uninspired bars offering a limited range of dull beers and food aimed at ageing couch potatoes, its fish & chip shops are giving way to seafood bistros, snack bars to bodegas, and B&Bs to boutique hotels. Even the dodgy jewellery shops have morphed into nicer-looking dodgy jewellery shops.

Spanish wine is everywhere but as yet no Spanish craft beer. Occasional cans from BrewDog and bottles from Cornwall's St Austell and Co. Carlow's O'Hara, appear, plus some oddities in chain restaurants contracted to foreign suppliers. At my last visit the most promising beer list was at **The Yard** (13B Ocean Village Marina – Fr-Sa 09.00-02.00; others 09.00-01.00), an attractive floating bar better known for its gins.

NEED TO KNOW

As a bite-sized community, cut off from the rest of global culture by sun, sea and Spain, expect to find endless local ways that are reminiscent of Torquay in the 1970s.

Accommodation: Churchill preferred the old-school Rock Hotel. The rest is transforming in line with a new economy.

Getting around: With the exception of its main attraction, Gibraltar is mostly flat, so walking is feasible. Six bus routes go everywhere except up to the Rock or its nature reserve.

Food: Gibraltar's cuisine is in transit. Rissoles and milky instant coffee are evolving into burgers and macchiato. Authentic paella and increasingly well-made international options can be found along Queensway Quay, Ocean Village Marina and Cornwall's Yard.

Hints: The border with Spain closes occasionally, each side blaming the other for this. When the prevailing south-westerly wind hits Force 6 it can bring the wrong sort of rain, diverting your plane to Málaga, an hour and a half away.

ABOUT HAMBURG

- **Population:** 1,780,000

- **Local breweries:** Gröninger and Blockbräu (heritage); Kehrwieder, Ratsherrn, Buddelship, Wildwuchs, Landgang and others (craft).

- **Trains:** Centrally located Hamburg Hbf station has direct connections with Berlin (±20 a day; 1.45-3 hours); Bamberg (±8 a day; 4.5-4.8 hours); and Copenhagen (±4 a day; 4.5-5 hours); via Duisberg or Osnabrück to Amsterdam (±8 a day; ±6 hours); and via Köln to Brussels (±8 a day; 6.5-7 hours).

- **Airport:** Hamburg airport is in the north of the city and has direct connections with Heathrow, Gatwick, Stansted and Manchester. The S-bahn S1 train connects every 10 minutes with Hamburg Hbf, takes 25 minutes and costs €3.30 each way, with a change to U-bahn U1 possible at Ohlsdorf. Taxis cost €25-30 each way.

- **Currency:** Euro (€)

HAMBURG

Germany's second largest city has evolved in recent years from a place of old dockyards, sleazy maritime street life and solid but lacklustre brewing, into one of striking waterfront architecture and a growing beer culture, second only to Berlin in national importance in many ways, though all is to some extent a work in progress.

While boasting no typical local beer style, its newer, more experimental local brewers are not averse to dabbling in lesser-known north and east German styles, such as Gose, Grätzer (Grodzisk), Lichtenhainer and Adambier, though their variations on more mainstream craft staples on the Pale Ale and Porter-Stout spectra are easily found.

The port city was famously the place where the Beatles – well, three of them – learned their trade in 1960, allegedly playing 48 consecutive nights at the Indra Club on Große Freiheit. Reeperbahn, the street at the heart of the St. Pauli district, has toned down its traditional trades in favour of peddling other forms of overblown tat, though its claim to be the heart of the city's nightlife remains true.

However, it is the harbours and many waterfronts along the river Elbe that are Hamburg's real attraction, such as the HafenCity quarter and the old Speicherstadt warehouse district, where the buildings sit above the water on oak piles. It spreads as far as the fishing village of Finkenwerder, which is also home to Airbus.

BEER VENUES

Little of Hamburg survived bombing by the RAF and its allies in 1943, so all of the following reflect the modern beer world. For something a little more traditional try the **Blockbräu** (Bei den St. Pauli-Landsbrücken 3 – block-braeu.de – daily 11.00-24.00) or **Gröninger Braukeller** (Willy-Brandt-Straße 47 – groeninger-hamburg.de – Mo-Fr from 11.00; Sa from 17.00; Su 15.00-22.00) older style brewery taphouses.

▶ CRAFT BIER BAR

Max Brauer Allee 275 – craftbierbar.de – shut Su; Mo-Sa 17.00-24.00 – S11, S21, S31: Holstenstraße

One of a small chain of north German bars, featuring a lengthy bottle list and 30 taps, with some self-pours. Well-chosen across a wide range of styles, with many local breweries featuring alongside other small-scale talent from across Europe. No food. The naked space is populated with shuffleboard tables and some old arcade games.

▶ ALTES MÄDCHEN
🅕🅣🅘 Lagerstraße 28B – altesmaedchen.com – *daily 12.00-23.00 – S11, S21, S31 and U3: Sternschanze*

The upscale tavern and restaurant of the Ratsherrn brewery, next to Hamburg Messe conference centre and the Sternschanze transport hub, has 30 taps and a 70-bottle list, while the physical end of the brewery's on-line store nearby sells nearer 300. Between here and the last address, next to the Rote Flora 30-year squat, is the distinctly alternative Galopper des Jahres (Schulterblatt 73 – dreiundsiebzig.de – daily from 17.00) a good place for local ales.

▶ ALLES ELBE
🅕🅘 Hein-Hoyer-Straße 63 – alleselbe.de – *shut Su-Mo; Tu-Sa from 18.00 – U3: St. Pauli*

Battered by COVID but not yet beaten, the range of beers in this dusky bar three blocks north of Reeperbahn is so enticing that its own brews can be drowned by the rest, which come mostly from central European small independents. High-quality nibbles are big enough to keep you there but not to fill. There is a small beer garden in summer.

▶ MALTO
🅕🅘 Max-Brauer-Allee 88 - maltoshanghait.beer – *shut Su-Mo; Fr-Sa 17.00-01.30; Tu-Th 17.00-23.30 – train: Hamburg-Altona, or bus 15, 20, 25, 183: Gerichtstraße*

West of the centre but only a five-minute walk from Altona station is the taphouse for Shanghait brewery, a sort of German-Italian-craft fusion brewery, with hazy beers and sharp food to match. Plainly furnished with a small courtyard area, its list of ten taps, with a couple of dozen bottles, is virtually all indie and full of interest.

▶ BREWDOG ST. PAULI
🅕🅘 Reeperbahn 1 - brewdog.com/bars – *Fr-Sa 12.00-02.00; Su-Th 12.00-24.00 – U3: St. Pauli*

BrewDog, the UK's most successful new

brewery in over a century, now has a brewery in Berlin and an international chain of bar franchises where they sell their own beers, usually alongside those of handpicked local brewers. Craft era fast food abounds. Many of the other destinations have one. The Hamburg outlet features for its location and address.

► BEYOND BEER

⌾ Weidenallee 55 – beyondbeer.de – shut Su; Sa 10.00-20.00; Mo-Fr 13.00-20.00 – U2: Christuskirche

Hamburg's leading beer shop is a well-lit, clearly laid out emporium of beery greatness, with a small sampling area, tastings on Thursday, and a great range of beers. This includes an ever-rolling selection of brews from top craft and heritage producers, and if you don't want to haul stuff around, they will ship orders to most of Europe.

NEED TO KNOW

One elegant but lazy way to view the river Elbe is to take some beers or book to dine at Störtebeker Elbphilharmonie (Platz der Deutchen Einheit 3 – stoertebeker-eph.com – Fr-Su 09.30-24.00; Mo-Th 11.30-24.00), the riverside restaurant-bar of 'the Elphi' concert hall. Better is to take ferry line 62 from Landungsbrücken to Finkenwerder, possibly wandering back along the Elbpromenade footpath. The Maritime Museum is worth a peek, and there are Beatles tours for those who must.

🛏 **Hotels:** Prices vary enormously but so do facilities and neighbourhoods. Because the transport system is so good, staying anywhere near a U3 'circle line' station is viable. Each to their own but I prefer the station side to St. Pauli.

🚌 **Getting around:** A day ticket from HVV (hvv.de) for zones A and B, valid from 09.00 to 06.00 on weekdays, or all day at weekends, includes all S-bahn and U-bahn trains, buses and the six harbour ferry lines in the city. It costs €6.90, with a group ticket for up to 5 people costing €12.90 and single fares €3.50. The Hamburg Card adds discounts on 150 sites.

🍴 **Food:** The German pork, potatoes and cabbage takes third place in this port city to the whole fish and seafood thing, and to the food implications of being a country's cosmopolitan second city. True authenticity demands eel soup (Aalsuppe), or a pickled herring and gherkin bap. A Hamburger is the name for a citizen (inedible).

⭐ **Hints:** For all its thick make-up and studied edginess, the St. Pauli area still has pickpockets and sneak thieves, so take basic precautions.

HAMBURG

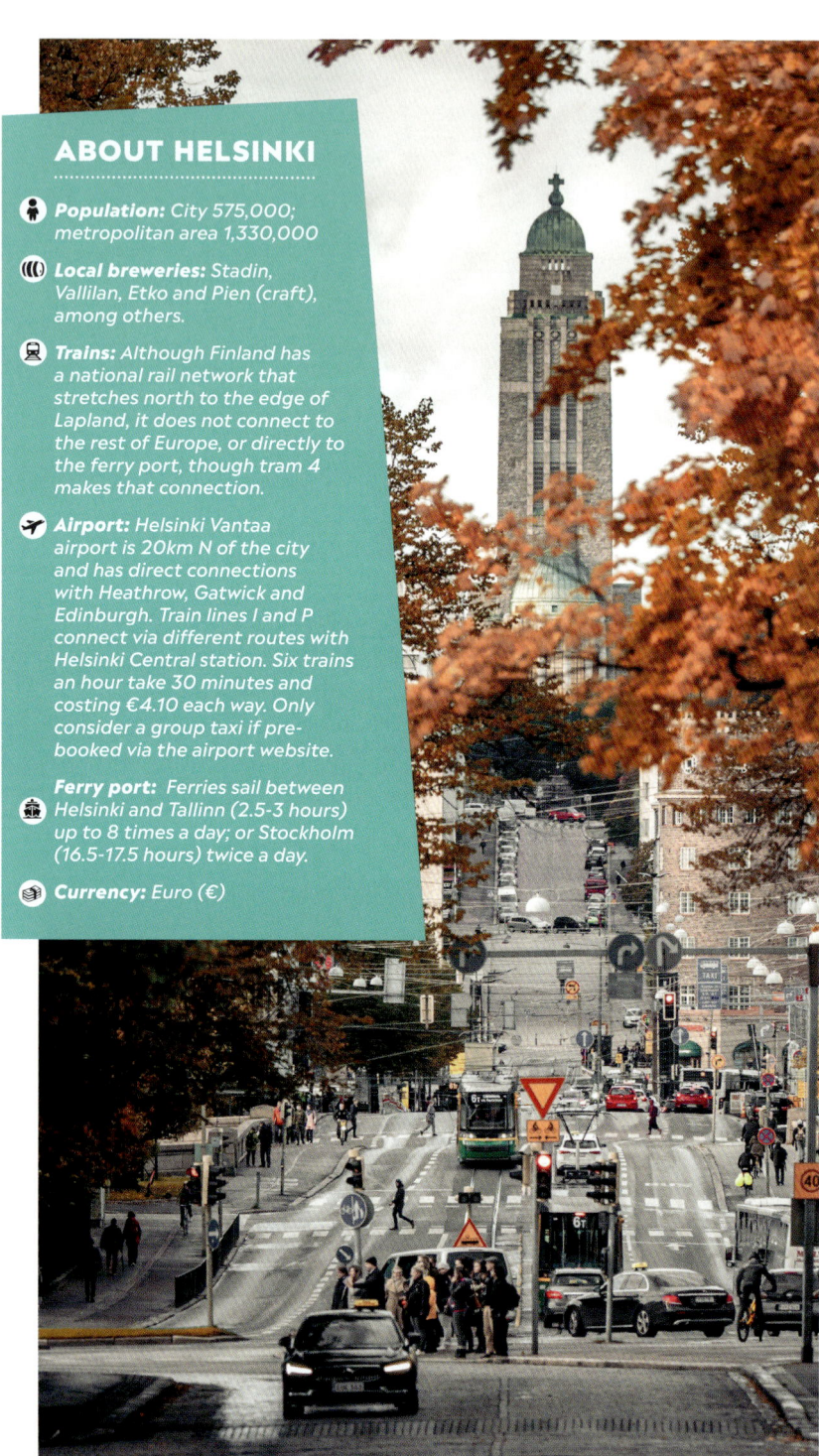

ABOUT HELSINKI

- **Population:** City 575,000; metropolitan area 1,330,000

- **Local breweries:** Stadin, Vallilan, Etko and Pien (craft), among others.

- **Trains:** Although Finland has a national rail network that stretches north to the edge of Lapland, it does not connect to the rest of Europe, or directly to the ferry port, though tram 4 makes that connection.

- **Airport:** Helsinki Vantaa airport is 20km N of the city and has direct connections with Heathrow, Gatwick and Edinburgh. Train lines I and P connect via different routes with Helsinki Central station. Six trains an hour take 30 minutes and costing €4.10 each way. Only consider a group taxi if pre-booked via the airport website.

- **Ferry port:** Ferries sail between Helsinki and Tallinn (2.5-3 hours) up to 8 times a day; or Stockholm (16.5-17.5 hours) twice a day.

- **Currency:** Euro (€)

HELSINKI

Finland has 187,888 lakes. The fact that these have been tightly defined and then counted is what matters. The number changes from time to time because they can merge, grow or disappear. Checking the number also says something important.

After independence from the Russian Empire in 1917, the Finns imposed Prohibition on themselves and did not lift it until 1932, despite it having brought a tsunami of smuggling and organised crime. They remain concerned about their propensity to drink too much and continue to impose rules that include restricting the sale of wines, spirits and stronger beers to a state-run chain of liquor stores called Alko.

Helsinki is Nordic rather than Scandinavian. While northern European, it is culturally unique in many ways. Its buildings will withstand anything nature throws at them, as will the locals.

Understanding its past means visiting UNESCO-protected Suomenlinna Fortress island. To see its future visit the central library, Oodi, for a coffee and the top-floor view. A trip to the Seurasaari Open-Air Museum introduces the rest of the country.

BEER VENUES

Finns drink 85% of their beer at home, including on nights when the habit of ottaa pohjat has them loading up before venturing out to the pub. It avoids unnecessary expense. With that important exception, Helsinki's pub culture has strong similarities with the UK's.

▸ PIKKULINTU RUTTOPUISTOR

ⓘ Lönnrotinkatu 11 – pikkulintu.fi – *Fr-Sa 12.00-02.00; Su-Th 15.00-24.00 – tram 6, 7, 9: Simonkatu; metro: Kampin*

For 20 years the most unlikely beer bar in Europe, Pikkulintu, was to be found in a dull shopping precinct on the outskirts of Helsinki. With its demolition, 'The Little Bird' has moved to a less well-worn but easier to find venue in the centre, to keep on serving its imaginative range of well-chosen beers from all over, plus some fabulous whiskies.

PIKKULINTU RUTTOPUISTOR

▶ KAISLA

🕐🍴 **Vilhonkatu 4 – raflaamo.fi**
– *daily from 13.00 – tram 3, 6, 9: Kaisaniemenkatu; metro: University*

One of the capital's longest standing beer bars now has 30 taps and a bottled list of up to 200, likely the longest in the centre. There are good wines too, and a menu of Finnish 'tapas', all served up in a pubby atmosphere. Its entrances sit either side of the Sori Taproom (soritaproom.com - shut Su; Mo-Sa 11.00-24.00), showcasing beers from the Finnish-owned Estonian brewery, alongside a menu with a few healthier options.

▶ ONE PINT

🕐 **Santakatu 2 – onepintpub.com**
– *Fr-Sun from 13.00; Mo-Th from 15.00 – tram 6, 7, 9: Länsilinkki*

This strangely comforting, battered old pub on the edge of the centre has been at the vanguard of promoting great beer in Finland since the beginning. Don't expect frills or food or even peace and quiet. Do expect a clever range of up to 100 beers from home and abroad, mostly from small independents, with 7 on draught. Bands play monthly.

▶ BIER-BIER

🕐🍴 **Erottajankatu 13 – bier-bier.fi** – *shut Su; Fr-Sa 14.00-02.00; Mo-Th 16.00-24.00 – tram 10: Kolmikulma or 1, 3: Erottja*

This place divides opinion. What is not in doubt is that it is dark and elegant, serves a large and imaginative range of Finnish and foreign beers and has some decent snacks. What bugs people is that even for a city where beer is expensive, it is pretty expensive, and that pre-COVID it tended to heave at busy times. It is an odd duet of problems.

▶ KITTY'S

🕐🍴 **Keskuskatu 6 – raflaamo.fi**
– *Fr-Sa from 11.00; others from 12.00 – tram 3, 6, 7, 9: Rautatieasema; metro M1, M2: Rautatientorin*

This openly pro-British pub, found just inside a shopping mall, has distinct ground floor and cellar levels. The Finns have respected British beer since the days of Baltic Porter and the range here tops 40, including one or more cask ales, in a range of ±70. Similar iterations of the British pub include polished Black Door (Iso Roba 1 – blackdoor.fi – daily from 12.00) and St. Uhro's (Museokatu 10 – uhrospub.fi – daily from 15.00), where sahti may be found.

▶ ALKO ARKADIA

🍶 **Salomonkatu 1** – *shut Su; Mo-Sa 09.00-21.00 – tram 1, 2, 4, 10: Lasipaltsi; metro M1, M2: Rautatientorin*

The chain of state-owned liquor stores is the only outlet, apart from brewery shops, allowed to sell beers of over 5.5% ABV for take-home, making Alko the biggest single market for small independent breweries in Finland. This is the best in the city, four minutes' walk from central station and carrying ±450 bottled or canned beers.

PIKKULINTU RUTTOPUISTOR

ONE PINT

NEED TO KNOW

Finland is a bilingual nation. For about 300,000 of its 5.5 million people, mostly along its southwestern and far western coasts, Swedish is their first language. In Helsinki (Helsingfors in Swedish) names often appear in both languages, equally incomprehensible to English-speakers and thus doubly confusing.

Accommodation: Seasons vary but the centre is expensive year-round and exorbitant in summer. Make huge savings by staying in a suburban apartment near to a station with a fast train connection to the centre.

Getting around: The metro is fully integrated into the train network, though the city's trams, the only ones in Finland, are usually the way to go. A joined-up 80-minute single ticket across all forms of public transport, including buses and the ferry to Suomenlinna, costs €2.80. Most tourism is found in travel Zones A or B. AB day cards from HSL (hsl.fi) cost €8 for 24 hours, with a €4 supplement for every 24 hours thereafter, up to 13 days.

Food: Delight in seriously expensive seafood or tolerate the glutinous sausages that save impoverished and unfussy carnivores from starvation. Pork dishes are common, beef less so. Designer vegetarian and vegan are easy to find. Putting berries and jams onto savoury dishes is classically Finnish.

Hints: Tipping is considered mildly insulting, so don't. Buying a round of drinks is seen as a donation rather than a favour to be repaid.

ABOUT LJUBLJANA

- **Population:** 275,000
- **Local breweries:** Loo-blah-nah, Omnivar and Tektonik, among others.
- **Trains:** Although Ljubljana station is well connected to the Balkans there are no direct connections to any other destinations in this book.
- **Airport:** Ljubljana airport is 24km N of the city and still a work in progress, its only current direct UK connections being Gatwick and Luton. The best connection with the city is to book a shuttle in advance via the airport website. The regular bus is slow and infrequent and the taxis unreliably priced.
- **Currency:** Euro (€)

LJUBLJANA

Ljubljana has one of the most striking townscapes in Europe, thanks to visionary architect Jože Plečnik, who returned home in 1920 after success in Vienna and Prague to raise a new city after the old one fell to an earthquake in 1895. The banks of the Ljubljanica river are now draped with public buildings, impressively lit at night, many with a dedicated bridge.

Slovenia was the northernmost state in the federation known between 1918 and 1991 as Yugoslavia, though in contrast to the others it never considered itself Balkan. Rather it looks and feels part of central Europe – perhaps a province of Austria, sold off for having an extreme dialect.

Slovenia's place in the new world of beer is guaranteed by its hop farmers. The Styrian hop fields that spanned the border with southern Austria for centuries now only thrive on the Slovenian side, where independent hop growers have banded together to expand the number of strains being cultivated, perfecting them for an era of more hop-forward beers, climate change allowing.

The way this small, rather beautiful country sees its future can be judged by its enthusiasm to join the Eurozone in 2007 ahead of the other former Soviet states, its ban on smoking in bars, and its support of localism ahead of the corporate ideal.

BEER VENUES

For complicated reasons the Slovenian brewing scene was held back until about 2014 by unintended reins. Since then an explosion of small breweries has brought enough talent for things to have got seriously interesting. In addition to Ljubljana's local brews, look out for beers from Crazy Duck, Green Gold, Hopsbrew, Lobik, Maister, Mali Grad, Pelicon and Reservoir Dogs. There are good Croatian and Serbian beers around too.

▶ LAJBAH

🛈 🍴 Grudnovo nabrežje 15 – lajbah.si
– Sa-Su 11.00-22.00; Mon-Fr 10.00-22.00
– bus 2, 3, 11, 19, 27: Gorni trg

To the south of the centre, near the Hradeckega pedestrian bridge and next to the river, is the country's foremost beer

LAJBAH

SIR WILLIAM'S PUB

bar. Nicely decked out inside, with a suntrap terrace for better weather, it not only has 20+ beers on tap and ±130 in bottle, it is also mercifully burger-free and has a seasonal menu of much healthier than average food.

➤ CRAFT ROOM

🛈🍺 Krakovski nasip 16 – craftroom.si – *Sa-Su 12.00-18.00; Mo-Fr 12.00-19.00* – bus 2, 3, 11, 19, 27: Gorni trg

This small, elegant beer shop is at the southern end of the centre, on the opposite side of the bridge from Lajbah (above). It stocks over 300 bottles and has a handful of taps, with a good mix overall that includes much Slovenian and European, plus Megobrebi beers from Georgia. There are a couple of tables for hanging around, and minor snacks.

➤ ŽE V REDU PRIMOŽ

🛈🍺 Trubarjeva cesta 44 – pr.primozu. shop – *shut Su; Sa 11.00-14.00 & 17.00-20.00; Mo-Fr 12.00-20.00* – bus 5: Ilirska, or bus 13, 20: Zmajski most

One of half a dozen excellent beer shops in the city but the best for high-quality up-to-date advice on what is happening on the Slovenian scene, with many practical illustrations on sale to take away, or sample either in the small back room or on the even smaller terrace. In a cosmopolitan area for snacks.

➤ SIR WILLIAM'S PUB

🛈 Tavčarjeva ulica 8a – sirwilliamspub. webs.com – *Sa-Su 17.00-22.00; Mo-Fr 08.00-22.00* – bus 5, 13, 20: Tavčarjeva

Centrally located, this pioneering beer bar was founded in 1998. An august affair with dark wood, polished mirrors and padded leather banquettes, its list of a dozen taps and 130+ bottles includes Slovenian pioneer Human Fish, other local brewers, plus imports from the rest of the Balkans and much of Europe. Lots of teas but minor snacks only.

➤ ZA POPEN'T

🛈 Stari trg 5 – zapopent.si – *Su 15.00-20.00; Mo-Sa 12.00-20.00*

The standard of beer stores in this university and touristic city is high, not just for their selection but for the style of service – low key in a trustworthy kind of way. COVID saw this one major on its online business but as restrictions lift its opening hours are increasing. Good for beers from Slovenia, Croatia and the rest of the Balkans.

LAJBAH

▶ IRISH PUB

🛈 🍴 Prečna ulica 6 – irishpub-ljubljana.si – shut Mo; Tu-Su from 17.00 – bus 13, 20: Zmajski most

It is possible to find tired, old, formulaic Irish pubs in many parts of the world but this one differs for having 80 beers on an international list that includes six independent Slovenian breweries plus some better performing British and Belgian ones. Ironically no Irish ones, except for O'Hara's occasionally. Pub-style fast food only.

NEED TO KNOW

Ljubljana is a great city for exploring. Of Plečnik's many architectural contributions, the National & University Library, the Central Market and Church of St Michael are the grandest, but if you visit just one, make it the man's own home on Karunova street. At the other end of the elegance spectrum, Metelkova Mesto is a former military barracks that is now a semi-autonomous urban enclave for those who regret missing hippiedom.

🛏 **Accommodation:** Try to stay within easy walking distance of the Old Town, or near the river. Prices are generally below the European average and standards high.

🚌 **Getting around:** The city is small enough to walk everywhere, though its cycling network is unusually advanced and bicycle hire is cheap and easy. The only alternative is the bus, which involves buying an Urbana card for €2 from the tourist office, bus station or any kiosk, and then topping it up by €1.30 per city journey, which can last up to 90 minutes.

🍴 **Food:** Don't leave town without becoming familiar with the state-protected smoked sausage Kranjska klobasa; sweet or savoury-filled rolled štruklji; the vegetable stew yota; and the egg-drop soup called prežganka. It's either that or yet more bloody burgers and pizzas.

⭐ **Hints:** Tipping is only for guilty tourists and should never go above 10%. Slovenes are not nationalist – they just think it's cool to be Slovenian.

LUXEMBOURG

CAMRA is a campaigning organisation formed mostly of volunteers. In this campaigning spirit I give you Luxembourg: not quite as poor a place as Gibraltar, but still a challenge.

The city draws in over 100,000 people each work day to staff 'investment' businesses that enable large corporations and extremely wealthy individuals to avoid the tax obligations that might beset them elsewhere.

On the upside, the nation and its capital invest their own taxes considerably, the former providing free public transport throughout the country, the latter free wi-fi in the city. On the downside, the beer culture is impoverished, the more so when contrasted with neighbouring Belgium, Germany and France.

That said, the city can be enjoyed. The old centre and its fortress are UNESCO World Heritage Sites, with 17km of tunnels carved into the soft rock beneath, also spectacularly eroded by the rivers Alzette and Pétrusse over millennia to create a city of two levels, best viewed from the Corniche above, and experienced from below at river and nightlife level in Grund.

ABOUT LUXEMBOURG

Population: 125,000

Trains: Luxembourg Gare Centrale has direct connections with Paris (±6 a day; 2,2 hours); and Brussels (±5 a day; 3.3 hours); or change in Koblenz for Hamburg (±6 a day; 7.6 hours).

Airport: Luxembourg Airport is 4km E of the city and has direct connections with Heathrow, Gatwick and Stansted. The centre is 15 minutes away by free Bus 16.

Currency: Euro (€)

BEER VENUES

Your role in helping Luxembourg to become as good a place for beer lovers as it was in the 19th century may be helped by the entries below, plus the good food and adequate house brews at Big Beer Company (12 Rives de Clausen – bigbeercompany.lu).

➤ THE STORE

🍴🍺 11 Avenue de la Liberté – thestore.rocks – *shut Su-We; Th-Sa 12.00-22.00 – tram T1: Place de Metz*

The ground-breaking Artisan'Ale moved upmarket and uphill in 2020, changing its name in the process but remaining the most accessible source of great beers in the city. There are a dozen taps and 200 bottles, plus a few chairs and tables in a tasting area that attracts the city's beer enthusiasts and others in the know.

➤ CRAFT CORNER

🍴🍺 112 Rue de Bonnevoie – craftcorner.lu – *shut Su; Sa 14.00-24.00; Th-Fr 16.00-24.00; Mo-We 16.00-23.00 – bus 3, 5, 6, 7, 27, 30, 32: Bonneville Léon XIII*

This self-declared gastro bar, one block behind the back of Gare Centrale, has a dozen beers on tap and ± 30 in bottles and cans from European craft brewers. It also has a nanobrewery at the back, called Bouneweger, for which it is currently the only outlet. Good food used to appear in all sizes before COVID and I assume will do so again.

➤ HOPPYLICIOUS

🍺 11 Avenue de Porte-Neuve – hoppy.lu – *shut Su-Mo; Sa 11.00-17.00; Tu 12.00-17.00; others 11.00-13.30 & 14.00-18.00 – train to Bertrange, then bus 255: Capellen Hirebesch*

Pre-COVID, the country's best store for locally brewed beers was 45 minutes free bus ride from town in the Parc d'Activités de Capellen. More recently I understand this branch has opened in the city centre. Either way, the company will deliver any order over €75 for free to anywhere in the country.

➤ UM TENNIS

🍴🍺 2 Rue Romains, Senningerberg – brasserie-um-tennis.lu – *shut Mo-Tu; Su 11.00-19.30; Tu-Sa 12.00-22.00 – bus 29, 120: Senningberg Charlys Statioun*

The only other ray of hope, strictly for explorers and those going for gold, is this bistro and beer bar next to a tennis club, out beyond the airport, reached by bus from there or Gare Centrale. Nice food, decent beers and you will get to see a little bit of the Luxembourg countryside.

NEED TO KNOW

Places that host a considerable wealth-preservation industry are often culturally bleak but the Grand Duchy tries its best to show an appreciation of the finer things in life.

- **Accommodation:** Often cheaper at weekends and tolerable in summer. Stay in the Old Town if it fits your budget.

- **Getting around:** Buses, trams and trains are all free.

- **Food:** Imagine German with a touch of Franco-Belgian and you are nearly there. Closest to national dishes are bouneschlupp (thick bean soup) and judd mat gaardebounen (smoked pork with broad beans).

- **Hints:** Tipping means nil or topping up. English is spoken widely. Best of luck with Lëtzeburgisch.

CRAFT CORNER

LUXEMBOURG

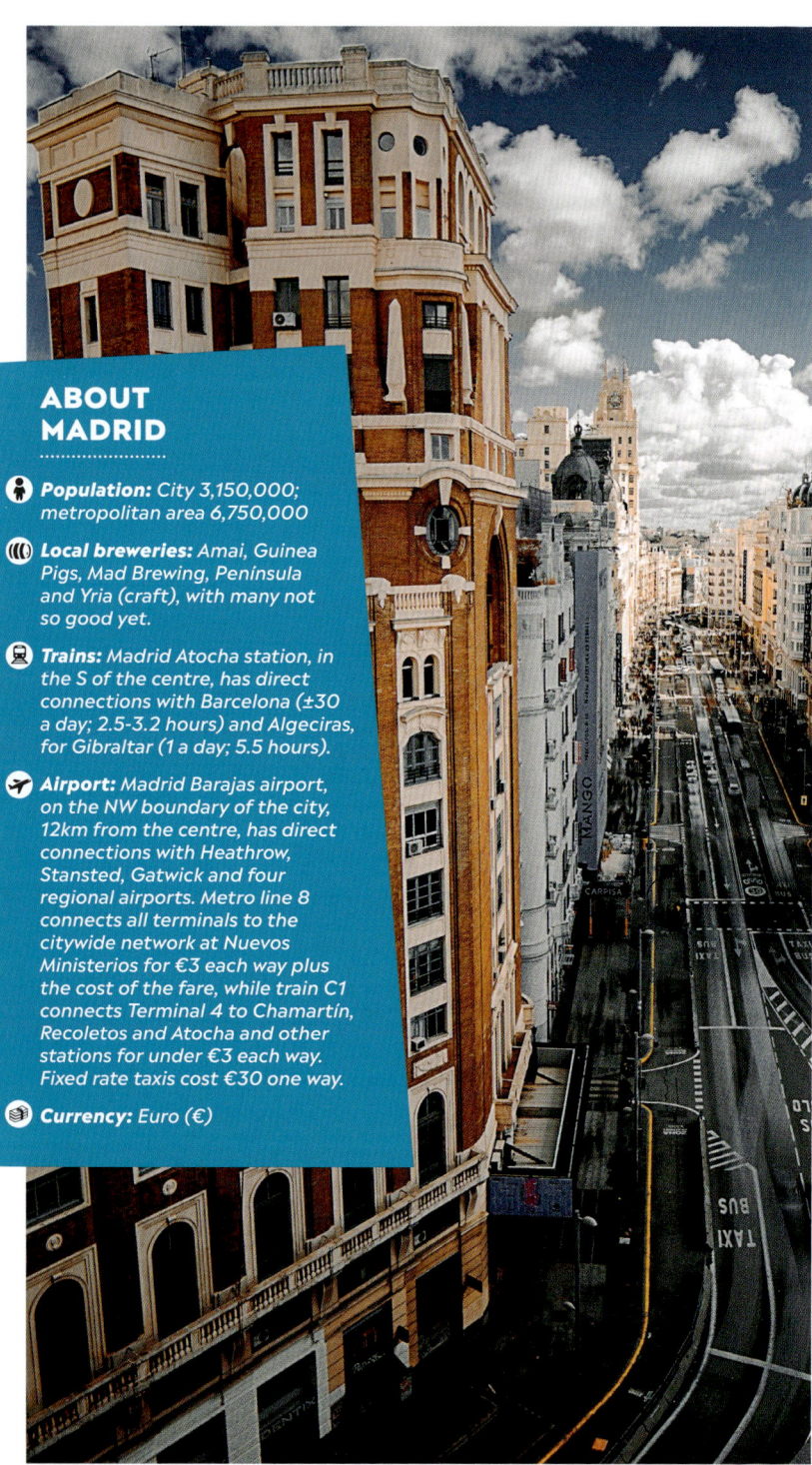

ABOUT MADRID

- **Population:** City 3,150,000; metropolitan area 6,750,000

- **Local breweries:** Amai, Guinea Pigs, Mad Brewing, Península and Yria (craft), with many not so good yet.

- **Trains:** Madrid Atocha station, in the S of the centre, has direct connections with Barcelona (±30 a day; 2.5-3.2 hours) and Algeciras, for Gibraltar (1 a day; 5.5 hours).

- **Airport:** Madrid Barajas airport, on the NW boundary of the city, 12km from the centre, has direct connections with Heathrow, Stansted, Gatwick and four regional airports. Metro line 8 connects all terminals to the citywide network at Nuevos Ministerios for €3 each way plus the cost of the fare, while train C1 connects Terminal 4 to Chamartín, Recoletos and Atocha and other stations for under €3 each way. Fixed rate taxis cost €30 one way.

- **Currency:** Euro (€)

MADRID

Madrid is huge, rivalling Berlin and Paris as the largest city in the EU. The Spanish capital is home to the great art collections of the Prado, Reina Sofía and Thyssen-Bornemisza museums, two famous football teams, Real and Atlético Madrid, the UN's World Tourism Organisation, and most of the big hitters in the Spanish economy.

Those who come here for the football often leave deflated, for the gallery tours quite the opposite. The Prado is among the world's largest and best curated museums, so choose which rooms to view before you go; the Thyssen-Bornemisza is one of the few galleries where you can walk through the whole story of European art; and Reina Sophia showcases flawlessly contemporary work from the last century.

Just as Paris came late to France's beer scene, so Madrid followed some way behind the new beer scenes in Catalonia, Galicia and the Basque country, though in the year before COVID Madrillenos were going beer crazy.

If it all gets too much and it's Sunday, head early to El Rastro junkfest, or during the rest of the week find the more nuanced Mercado San Miguel – a mix of fresh produce and beautiful food stalls, with up-scale tapas, in a century-old Art Nouveau market hall.

BEER VENUES

The downside of establishing a major beer scene in a city like Madrid, where any new fad is the best thing for a time, is that start-ups are ill-equipped to survive a pandemic. Before going viral, so to speak, Madrid's lust for craft beer had only reached second base. For now at least, I recommend the following.

▶ FOGG

🛈 🍴 Calle de Moratin 5 – foggbar.es/birras-cheese – *shut Mo; Fr-Sa 19.00-24.00; Tu-Th 19.00-23.30 – metro 1: Antón Martín*

The largest Madrilleno beer bar listed here has a well-worn feel, like the sort of early 20th century, wood-lined long bar once found in most European capitals. The 10 beers on tap are backed by a menu of ±100 bottles. The other speciality is the great range of intense hard cheeses, Iberian ham and dried sausage, worth sampling even with a limonada.

▶ CHINASKI LAVAPIÉS
🛈 Calle de la Fe 19 – chinaskilavapies.com – *Sa-Su from 13.00; Mo-Fr from 18.00 – metro 3: Lavapiés*

By the church of San Lorenzo, on the corner of Calle Salitre, this deceptively large, odd-shaped bar in a busy night-time area has pioneered beer in Madrid since 2015. Its painted walls are an acquired taste but its relentless downmarket vibe works. The beer list of ±80 beer favours the stronger, hazier and weirdly yeasted. Snacks are limited.

▶ CLBM BAR
🛈 🍴 Calle de las Huertas 59 – clbmbar.es – *shut Mo-Tu; We-Th 19.00-24.00; Fr 18.00-01.00; Sa-Su 13.00-17.00 & 19.00-01.00 – metro 1: Antón Martín*

A short, winding walk from Fogg (above), this simply designed Como La Birra Misma ('Like The Beer Itself') has already built a strong following for its 100% indie list of 14 taps and 50+ bottles-cans, inevitable burgers and high calorie salads.

▶ BREW WILD
🛈 🍴 Calle de Echegaray 23 – brewwildmadrid.com – *daily from 13.00 – metro 1: Antón Martín, metro 2: Sevilla, or metro 3: Sol*

In a pedestrian enclave equidistant and seven minutes' walk from three metro lines, this pizzeria and beer bar has a smallish street-level bar for vertical drinking and a stone-floored cellar with exposed walls for food and chat. Its 18 taps and well-stocked fridge include interesting stuff from smaller European indies and co-owners La Quince.

▶ LA TIENDA DE LA CERVEZA
🛈 🛒 🍴 Calle de las Maldonadas 12 - FB/LaTiendaDeLaCerveza – *Mo 18.00-24.00; Tu-Su 12.00-24.00 – metro 5: La Latina*

Many of the pretentious places that sell good beer in Madrid are full of sanctimonious marketing hooey. This place, one minute from La Latina metro, is the antidote. A straight-up bar with take-home, run by helpful hosts, serving simple plain and decent food, has the atmosphere of a Spanish-style community pub that likes to sell great beer.

▶ LA BUENA CERVEZA

🛈 ♿ Calle de Hernán Cortés 7 - labuenacerveza.com – *shut Su; Mo-We 13.00-23.00; Th-Sa 13.00-24.00* – *metro 5: Chueca, or metro 1, 10: Tribunal*

This compact but well-stocked beer shop, with a small bar area, differs from the many others operating in the city for weaving strong threads of new Spanish brewing into a range of better European and North American imports. Their website details the beer list and delivery options but not their well-reported tasting classes.

NEED TO KNOW

Madrid's tourist year runs cheap and cold (Dec-Feb), modest and balmy (Mar-May), expensive and unbearable (Jun-Aug), then reasonable and best (Sep-Nov).

🛏 **Accommodation:** Because Madrid is so huge, hotels and apartments of all standards abound. Aim for Centro, the Centre, or else somewhere within an easy metro ride of it.

🚌 **Getting around:** There are two ways of doing this. The cheaper is strictly for locals with a lot of patience, and can be researched via the transport company's website (metromadrid.es). The second is to pay up a bit of tourist tax and buy an Abono Turístico travel pass, allowing unlimited trips on the metro, trams, urban trains and buses within the central zones A and T. These are valid for 1, 2, 3, 4, 5 or 7 days, up to 05.00 the following day, and cost between €8.40 and €35.40 depending on the number of days, or double that to cover the whole of greater Madrid. Best stick to the metro.

🍴 **Food:** The Spanish have distinctive eating habits. Lunch (comida) is typically between 14.00 and 15.30 and dinner (cena) between 21.00 and 23.00. Hence tapas, the perfect get-out clause for snackers, found in all sizes and forms.

⭐ **Hints:** As a general rule only tourists tip, though topping up is common. The gesture made by creating an O by linking the tips of thumb and index finger means 'I am up for a drink' – I hope.

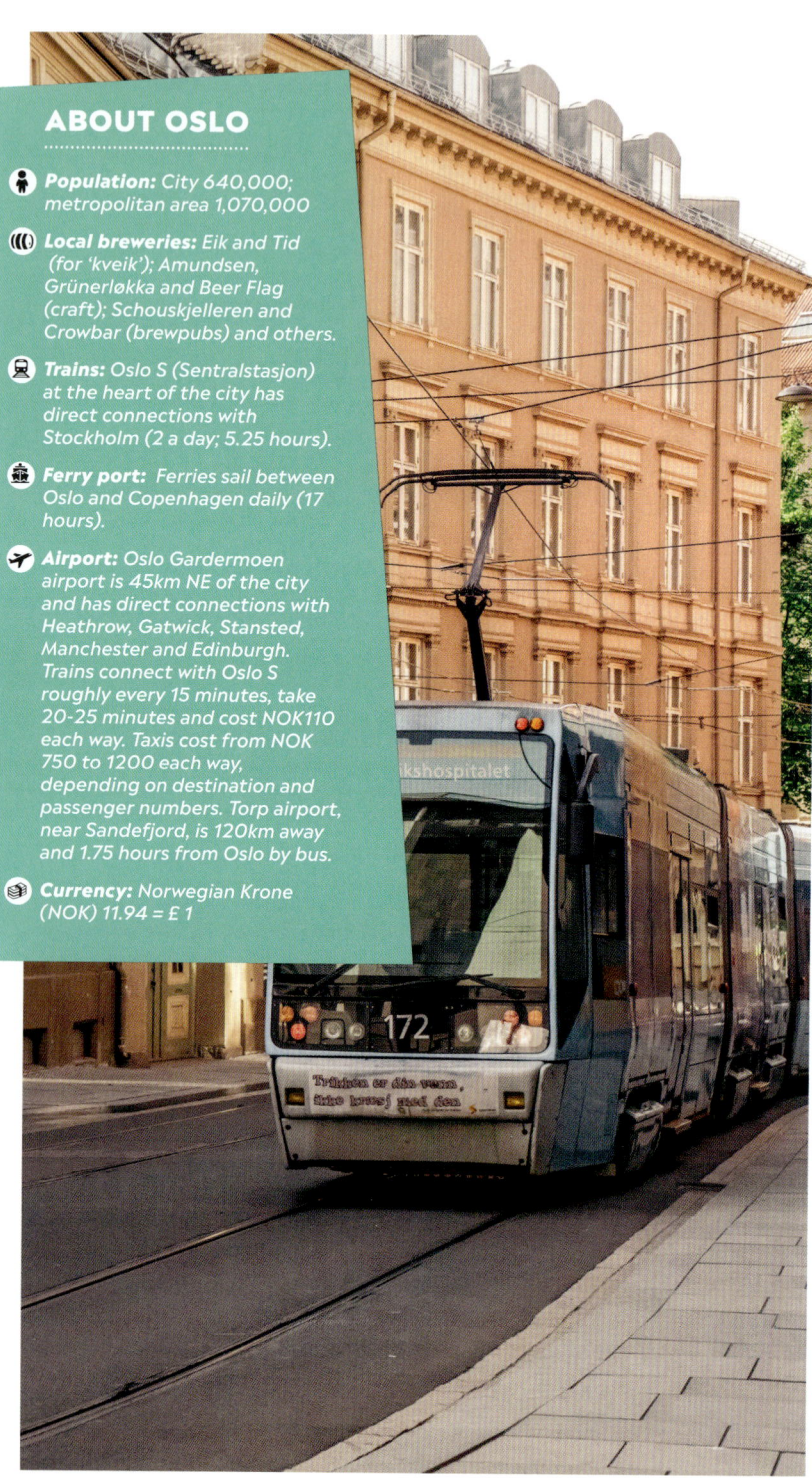

ABOUT OSLO

- **Population:** City 640,000; metropolitan area 1,070,000

- **Local breweries:** Eik and Tid (for 'kveik'); Amundsen, Grünerløkka and Beer Flag (craft); Schouskjelleren and Crowbar (brewpubs) and others.

- **Trains:** Oslo S (Sentralstasjon) at the heart of the city has direct connections with Stockholm (2 a day; 5.25 hours).

- **Ferry port:** Ferries sail between Oslo and Copenhagen daily (17 hours).

- **Airport:** Oslo Gardermoen airport is 45km NE of the city and has direct connections with Heathrow, Gatwick, Stansted, Manchester and Edinburgh. Trains connect with Oslo S roughly every 15 minutes, take 20-25 minutes and cost NOK110 each way. Taxis cost from NOK 750 to 1200 each way, depending on destination and passenger numbers. Torp airport, near Sandefjord, is 120km away and 1.75 hours from Oslo by bus.

- **Currency:** Norwegian Krone (NOK) 11.94 = £ 1

OSLO

Oslo is a classic northern European city, compact in a way that befits a place where people hunker down in winter, yet keen to open up in summer via its waterfront. Taxes are high, along with prices and wages, and there is political will to keep beer expensive. Norwegians here in the capital tolerate the wildly expensive nature of partying.

When Nøgne Ø broke into the Norwegian beer world in 2004, they reasoned that they could not compete on cost so would do so on quality. If bars sold small glasses of average Pilsner for £5, they would make large bottles of sipping beers, like a 9% Imperial Stout, to sell at £15. It was a massive risk but it worked. Today's sour, sweet and extract-laced beers are minor in comparison.

For tourism take bus 30 to the Norsk Folkemuseum of reconstructed historical buildings on the Bygdøy peninsula, then descend the hill via four others — dedicated to 9th century Viking ships; the Kon-Tiki and Ra expeditions of Thor Heyerdahl; Roald Amundsen's polar exploration ship the Fram; and the rest of Norway's rich maritime heritage — before returning by pay-for ferry.

Find art in the Munch Museum – for 'The Scream' – and the indoor and outdoor statuary of Vigeland Park and Museum.

BEER VENUES

Alcohol and dining are expensive here, but trying to save by drinking cheaper beers is a false economy. The trick is to buy the best beers in the best places but then sip, not gulp. In the case of the more challenging recreation of oddly yeasted 'farmhouse' beers, sipping is also good.

▶ CAFÉ SARA

ℹ️🍽 Hausmannsgate 29 - cafesara.no
– Su 13.00-03.30; others 11.00-03.30 – bus 34, 54: Jakob Kirke

North of the station is this pleasantly old-style street corner bar with a large courtyard at its rear. Famed for its huge range of better value grills and fast food, served till 02.30, it also stocks a dozen beers on tap and a host of bottles. Just up the way is the Crowbar brewpub (Torggata 32 - Sa 13.00-03.00; others 15.00-03.00).

▶ RØØR

ℹ️ Rozenkrantzgate 4 - roor.no
– Fr-Sa 13.00-03.00; Su-Th 15.00-01.00
– tram 11, 17, 18: Tinghuset

Possibly the best draught beer selection in Europe, right in the heart of the city. The array of up to 70 taps in the huge ground-floor bar complements a decent wine list and whisky selection. The first floor has a gin bar, minimum age 20, while the top floor houses 14 shuffleboard tables that can be hired for NOK 300 each per hour.

▶ HOPYARD

🛈 Mathallen, Vulkan 5 – hopyard.no
– *shut Mo; Su 12.00-20.00; Fr-Sa 11.00-00.30; Tu-Th 11.00-23.30 – bus 34, 54: Møllerveien*

It takes a bit of effort to find this excellent beer bar, set in the Mathallen food and crafts market, an 8-minute walk from the previous entry. Choose from over 200 beers, a large proportion from small Norwegian independents, with a few choice imports, helped by knowledgeable servers. Home-made snacks have appeared since my last visit.

▶ SCHOUSKJELLEREN MIKROBRYGGERI

🛈 Trondheimsveien 2 – FB/Schoukjelleren – *Fr from 15.00; others from 16.00 – tram 11, 12, 17: Heimdalsgata*

This cult beer venue is first and foremost a brewpub, despite the wide range of other

LORRY

BEER BREAKS

brewers' beers on the 20 taps and long list. Being based in an ancient if expansive cellar makes it warm and cosy in winter and cool in summer. Keeps on rolling till the wee small hours. No food.

▶ LORRY

🛈 🍴 Parkveien 12 - lorry.no
- Tu-Sa 11.00-03.30; Su 12.00-01.00; Mo 11.00-01.00 - tram 17, 18, 19: Welhavens gate

The first time I visited Oslo, in the late 1990s, this epically memorable, old-fangled restaurant, famed for its classical Norwegian cooking, stocked virtually every beer available from the country's much depleted handful of heritage brewers. Today, still spread over two high-ceilinged stories of upscale bric-a-brac emporium and spill-over terraces, the range of beers served is far wider, yet still a back-up act to the magnificence of its atmospherics and cuisine.

▶ VINMONOPOLET

🛈 Jernbanetorgget 1 – vinmonopolet.no
– shut Su; Sa 10.00-16.00; Mo-Fr 10.00-18.00 – Oslo S station

State-owned Vinmonopolet liquor stores are the only places in Norway licensed to sell beer of over 4.7% ABV for take-home. This one is conveniently located within Oslo S train station. Greater Oslo has around 30, most sharing the same opening hours. Stock varies but the website displays the current range and stock in each store.

Three others worth considering are **Olympen** (Grønlandsleiret 15 – olympen.no - shut Su-Mo; Sa 12.00-01.00; Tu-Fr from 11.00) for its summer courtyard, touch of swank and expensive but excellent restaurant menu; **Amundsen Bryggeri & Spiseri** (Stortingsgaten 20 - amundsenspiseri.no), where Oslo's most successful craft brewery began; and **Brygg** (Storgata 7 – brygg.no – Fr-Sa 12.00-24.00; Su 15.00-23.00; Mo-Th 14.00-24.00), for a lot of space in which to have fabulous beers and guided tastings.

NEED TO KNOW

Norwegians are by tradition God-fearing souls. Taken with moderation in all things, this is probably why so many stay healthy late into their remarkably long lives. The trappings of post-hipster modernity seen in Oslo's beer culture are a cultural aberration.

🛏 **Accommodation:** Prices vary enormously with the season and events, so be flexible and book well ahead. Aim for the centre, the waterfront, or just off a tram route.

🚋 **Getting around:** The tram, bus, metro and urban train networks share a single ticketing system, along with local ferries, except for those to Bygdøynes quay. For the city itself, a single 60-minute ticket costs NOK38, 24 hours NOK114 and 7-day NOK320.

🍴 **Food:** Norwegian food comes on three levels: the hot dog and meatball; the hearty stew; and the beautifully prepared and arranged fish or seafood thing, the last of which can be as beautiful as it is expensive. Then there is thin-sliced brunost (or gjetost) – where cheese meets fudge.

⭐ **Hints:** Norwegians only really tip in restaurants and even then, not always. Typical is 10% for decent service and 20% for exceptional. Do NOT fall asleep in a bar, or you and all those at your table must be asked to leave and not return before the following day.

LORRY

ABOUT PARIS

Population: City 2,180,000; metropolitan area 11,140,000

Local breweries: Grand Paris, Goutte d'Or, Fauve and Paname, among others.

Trains: Paris has numerous mainline stations. Montparnasse has direct connections with Bordeaux (±16 a day; 2.1-3.5 hours); Gare de l'Est with Luxembourg (±6 a day; 2.2-3 hours); and Gare du Nord with Brussels (±14 a day; 1.4-1.5 hours); Antwerp (±7 a day; 2.0 hours); Amsterdam (±7 a day; 3.3 hours); and via Eurostar to London St Pancras (<12 a day; 2.4-3.1 hours).

Airport: Paris Charles de Gaulle airport is 23km NE of the centre and has direct connections with most London and regional UK airports. The RER B train takes 35 minutes to link with Châtelet les Halles and costs €10 each way. Smaller, older Orly airport is 14km S of the centre and connects directly with seven regional UK airports but not London. It links by bus to Montparnasse in 30 minutes for €9.50 or via the Orlyval driverless shuttle to RER B train station Antony and on to the centre in 35 minutes from €12.10.

Currency: Euro (€)

PARIS

Capital cities usually lead beer revolutions. Not so Paris, which was way too cool and pompous for that kind of thing. The beer specialty here had been expensive – until suddenly malt became the way to go and la bière artisanale, preferably rustique, was accepted as an essential of Parisian life.

Always a young person's place, oldies will notice the absence of escalators and lifts. Sites like Gustav Eiffel's Tower, the Louvre, the Pompidou Centre or the Musée d'Orsay invariably have queues. Walking along the banks of the Seine at river level is still free, easy and mildly emboldening.

BEER VENUES

Put anything intended for the stomach into the hands of a French creative and they will play with it to make it better, or at least more memorable. So it is with bière artisanale, a term first heard here in the late 1960s. The average beer café stocks wheat beers, IPAs and sour stuff, with dollops of Stout and brews containing fruit extracts or spices. The latest trend is Czech lagers from small, independent Bohemian breweries.

▶ LA FINE MOUSSE

🛈 🍴 Avenue Jean Aicard – lafinemousse.fr – bar: Mo-Th from 17.00; Fr-Su from 16.00, restaurant: daily from 19.00, plus Sa-Su 12.00-14.30 – métro 3: Rue St Maur

To begin at the top, the bar part here is at No. 6 and sports ±20 taps from all over, plus 100+ bottled examples of post-modern French ales, while its must-reserve restaurant across the street at 4bis serves a short but excellent menu that brings out the best from a swanky, extended list of special beers in its 'cave'. They also run a superb, expensive, indulgently craft bar near Odéon called La Robe et La Mousse (3 Rue Monsieur le Prince – daily from 16.00) serving only the best in beers, organic wines and top-rate snacks.

▶ L'ATALANTE

🛈 🍴 26 Quai de la Marne – atalanteourcq.fr – Fr-Su from 12.00; Mo-Th from 17.00 – métro 5: Ourcq, or 7: Crimée

On a canal bank in a reclaimed part of the inner city, this cool bistro with a panoramic view of the waterway serves all sorts of craft drinks and a clever array of street food, where street means good, usually until 01.30, with 15-20 taps, half French, and as many bottles. First and foremost a local gathering place, it nonetheless welcomes all effortlessly.

LA FINE MOUSSE

LA FINE MOUSSE

▶ EXPRESS DE LYON
🛈🍴 1 Rue de Lyon – expresslyon.com
– *shut Su; Sa from 12.00; Mo-Fr from 09.00 – métro 1, 14: Gare de Lyon*

An unusually beery take on a classic French institution – the opposite-the-station bar. These quick-bite-and-a-beer establishments are often found side-by-side near train stations like Gare de Lyon. Some operate 24/7, though this one shuts around midnight. Its huge beer list features great French beers and a few better Belgians.

▶ HOPPY CORNER
🛈 34 Rue des Petits Carreaux – FB/hoppycorner
– *shut Su; Sa 14.00-02.00; Mon-Fr 17.00-02.00 – métro 3: Sentier*

A surprisingly rustic, little, long bar in the centre of the city, though particularly busy at weekends. Within a healthy walk of many attractions and transport hubs, it carries one of the best selections of beer in the city, with 15 taps and around 50 bottles. Totally dedicated to beer, with no food.

▶ BREWBERRY
🛈🍴 11 Rue Pot de Fer – FB/brewberrylebar – *shut Su-Mo; Tu-Sa from 17.00 – métro 7: Place Monge*

One of the rare examples of an entry I have not visited personally, being substituted last-minute for a bar that died from the reaction to COVID. It began as a beer store in 2014 then sprouted a bar with two dozen beers on tap and a huge bottled range, plus a menu and even wine list that draw praise. I hope it's good.

BEER BREAKS

L'ATALANTE

LA FINE MOUSSE

▶ À LA BIÈRE COMME À LA BIÈRE

🍺🕐 353 Rue des Pyrénées – alabierecommealabiere.com
– shut Su-Mo; Tu-Th 16.00-22.00; Fr-Sa 12.00-22.00 – métro 11: Jourdain

The second son of a small chain that have a smaller branch in Montmartre (20 Rue Coustine – shut Su-Mo; Fr-Sa from 12.00; Tu-Th from 16.00) and a bar out in Montreuil. Usually 500 beers in stock, with a small and eccentric tasting room at the back.

NEED TO KNOW

Paris is not currently the romantic city it was. Too edgy to feel safe and too privileged to be considered gritty, it can nonetheless still charm.

🛏 **Accommodation:** Hotels and apartments abound but vary in price and value considerably. Check out the neighbourhood before booking, then pick somewhere close to the Métro.

🚇 **Getting around:** The iconic 16-line, 300-station Métropolitain (Le Métro) is by far the easiest way to get around, though intersections are not its strong point. Its tickets also cover RER urban trains, trams and buses and cost €1.90 each or €18.60 for un carnet of 10. Paris Visite 1-, 2-, and 3-day passes include museums entry and so on but you have to sweat to make them worthwhile.

🍴 **Food:** Mon Dieu! Every third shop is a restaurant, and the types of cuisine cover the whole gamut from Mongolian to Moroccan. Old hands go for entrecôte frites, great things done with offal, anything billed as of regional origin, plus any cheese not seen before.

⭐ **Hints:** Tipping means topping up in bars, restaurants and taxis. Sadly, opportunist street crime is rife, especially on the Métro, so keep your bags close and closed, and put wallets and purses inside your clothing.

L'ATALANTE

PORTO

The hilly city of Porto, near the mouth of the Douro river and home to port wine and salt cod, was the crucible of Portuguese craft brewing. The first arrived in 2002 and a second, Sovina, in 2009. Before that Carlsberg-owned Super Bock dominated the north of the country, and Sagres (Heineken) the south. About half of today's 'brewers' have breweries, the rest relying on others to do the hard bit.

With a little research you can locate a dozen gaudy churches in Porto, a whole quay's worth of Vinho do Porto tasting rooms, and a collection of river bridges to rival Newcastle's. The Livraria Lello (Rua das Carmelitas 144) is such a cute bookshop that people queue to pay €5 to enter, refundable against a purchase.

ABOUT PORTO

- **Population:** City 250,000; metropolitan area 1,320,000
- **Local breweries:** Sovina, Colossus and others.
- **Airport:** Porto airport is 12km N of the city and has connections to four London and five regional airports. Metro line E connects with the centre two or three times an hour, takes half an hour and costs €2.45. Taxis cost roughly €40 each way.
- **Currency:** Euro (€)

CATRAIO

BEER BREAKS

BEER VENUES

Nearly 70% of beer in Portugal is consumed in bars, the highest proportion in Europe. Expect classic German, British and Belgian styles, adjusted to local tastes.

▶ CATRAIO

ℹ️🍺 Rua de Cedofeita 256 – catraio.pt – *shut Su-Mo; Fr-Sa 16.00-02.00; others 16.00-24.00 – tram 18: Carmo*

Craft beer central for northern Portugal is this top rate beer shop, where the tasting room has become a 15-tap bar, with a covered roof-level space, its tables set among trees. The beer selection tops 100, with brews sourced from all over Europe and very few duds. No food, and a seven-minute walk from the nearest tram stop but a must-visit.

▶ LETRARIA BEER GARDEN

ℹ️🍽️ Rua da Alagria 101 - cervejaletra.pt – *shut Tu; Su 16.00-23.00; others from 17.00 – metro A, B: Bolhão*

The local taphouse for Letra brewery of Vila Verde, not far from Bolhão market. Deceptively small at street level, its larger bar downstairs opens up onto a large, well-tended garden. 20+ taps from Letra and others, plus ±80 bottles. A few petiscos, though bigger food is variants on burgers. Opens daily in summer 11.00-02.00.

▶ ARMAZÉM DA CERVEJA

ℹ️🍺 Rua Formosa 130 - armazem.beer – *shut Mo; Fr-Sa 16.00-01.00; others 16.00-24.00 – metro A, B: Bolhão*

Around the corner, one block down from Letraria, is this far less calculated beer shop-cum-bar with a small yard at the back. It won't win awards for beauty or cosiness but does offer an eclectic range of ±150 beers, around 20% Portuguese, for drinking in or taking home. Serves a few nibbles and doesn't mind if you bring your own food.

▶ CERVEJARIA DO CARMO

ℹ️ Praça de Carlos Alberto 124 – FB/cervejariadocarmo – *daily from 13.00 – tram 18, 22: Carmo*

A three-minute, block-and-a-half, zigzag walk from Livraria Lello (above), is this plain but welcoming beer café and its streetside terrace. Beginning life as a brewpub it has progressed to become a reliable supplier of beers from around the country and beyond. The striking azulejo-tiled church on the corner is the Igreja do Carmo.

NEED TO KNOW

The local speciality is weather, with recent summers having been way too hot. Most attractions are open all year round and lodgings are way cheaper from November to March.

🛏️ **Accommodation:** Aim for the elevated part of the city centre or else reasonably close to a metro or train station to make getting around easier.

🚇 **Getting around:** The six-line metro is efficient, the trams are great and the funicular railway is touristic gold. An Andante card, from transport hubs, tourist offices and some hotels (€0.60), covers buses and urban trains too. Topping it up costs €1.20 for one journey, €10.80 for ten, €4.15 for 24 hours in the centre, or €7 for 24 hours, €15 for 72, including the airport. Taxis are cheap.

🍴 **Food:** In good value restaurants petiscos equate to tapas. Top local specialities include salt fish, octopus, spicy sausage, beans drowned in tomatoes, liquid spinach, suckling pig and slabs of beef cooked in various formats.

⭐ **Hints:** Only tip for great service and limit this to 5-10%. The locals favour tawny port, the finest being designated a Colheita.

ARMAZÉM DA CERVEJA

ABOUT PRAGUE

- **Population:** 1,320,000
- **Local breweries:** U Fleků (heritage), Únětický, Uhříněves, Sibeeria and Břevnovský Benedict (craft), and pre-COVID, over 40 brewpubs.
- **Trains:** Prague's Hlavní Nádraží station is in the city centre and has direct connections with Berlin (±6 a day: 4.7 hours); Vienna (±6 a day: 4.6-4.8 hours); and Budapest (±6 a day: 7.1-7.6 hours).
- **Airport:** Prague Vaclav Havel airport is 17km W of the city and connects with Heathrow, Gatwick, Stansted and six regional UK airports. The fastest public transport route to the centre is the frequent bus 119, which drops you onto the metro system at Nádraží Veleslavín (line A). Taxis to the Old Town cost around CZK700.
- **Currency:** Czech Koruna (CZK) 29 = £ 1

PRAGUE

It was in Prague in 1985, four years before the Velvet Revolution ended the Soviet occupation, that I first discovered why blond lager conquered the world of beer in the 20th century, how the humble dumpling could be weaponised, and the ways in which gentle humour can topple the fiercest of beasts.

Among Prague's many claims to fame is that of being the largest city in Bohemia, a part of the world that brought many firsts to brewing. It was around here that hops were first used routinely in brewing in the 9th century, that the first communal breweries were created in the 10th century, that ale was first successfully taxed in the 11th century, and where in 1842 the ancient art of lagering met its blond muse.

Bohemian pale lager, or světly, is the world's most complex simple beer. Its malt is coaxed by decoction mashing into giving up all its flavours, its balancing hops are bred to match perfectly, and its imperfections are massaged away by months of cold-conditioning. It has virtually nothing in common with its industrial equivalents, other than appearance.

For the finest světly ležák 12° – the fulsome grainy one – or světlé výčepní 10°, its slimmer little sister, glinting in a heavily-faceted, thick-glassed, half-litre pull, seek out upstart modern breweries like Únětický, Dalešice, Hendrych and Kácov, or the tank versions of original Pilsner Urquell, or Budejovické, the Czech Budweiser.

Prague is beautiful, well preserved and does great views. The Charles Bridge (Karlův Most) over the Vitava river is best seen at night, after tourist time. The Castle (Hrad) impresses best from afar. For a taste of the real Prague, head for the places I have recommended, and then go explore from there.

BEER VENUES

Prague has a draught beer and pub culture not unlike that found in the UK, though the Czechs drink two-thirds of their beer at home. Of the country's 400+ breweries, two-thirds are brewpubs. Names to look out for, not mentioned elsewhere, include Nomad, Antoš, Clock, Permon and Raven.

▶ U FLEKŮ

Křemencova 11 – en.ufleku.cz – *Fr-Sa 11.00-23.00; Su-Th 11.00-22.00 – tram 5: Myslíkova*

This 1200-seater, eight room, granite-built brewpub, with its internal beer garden and much darkened panelling, has likely been in continuous production for over 500 years, knocking out the archetypal dark Bohemian lager and standard Bohemian cooking. For this, rather than its prices, service, or ghastly sweet liqueur, it is a global bucket list collectable.

▶ U KUNŠTÁTŮ

🛈 🍴 Řetězová 3 – ukunstatu.cz – *daily 16.00-23.00 – metro & many trams: Staroměstská*

A beer bar like no other, in the centre of the pedestrianised Old Town but nicely off the beaten track. Welcome for its shaded summer courtyard, its unique feature is its Romanesque cellar and part-time art gallery. If the array of mostly bottled Czech beers flummoxes you, the frequent and bookable tutored tastings are good value. Interesting snacks too.

▶ PIVOVARSKÝ KLUB

🛈 🍴 Křižíkova 272 – pivoklub.cz – *Su 12.00-22.00; Mo-Sa 11.00-23.30 – metro & bus station: Florenc*

This street-level beer bar with food, and its downstairs restaurant, are lined with hundreds of beers and memorabilia and awash with conversation and conviviality. The six taps sell carefully chosen examples of high-quality Czech beer, with the range of ±240 bottles more international. Eating here is a good idea but you must book in the evening.

▶ ZLÝ ČASY

🛈 🍴 Čestmírova 390 – zlycasy.eu – *Su 17.00-01.00; Mo-Sa 15.00-02.00 – tram 2, 3, 4, 6, 7, 11, 13, 14, 17, 18, 21, 22, 24: Náměstí Bratří Synků*

PIVOVARSKÝ KLUB

PIVOVARSKÝ KLUB

'Hard Times' is a hard-working, three-story pub at the back of Vršovice train station, enjoying international acclaim for an extensive beer list, featuring small brewery beers of all formats, styles and origins. Its cellar bar is legendary. They serve a standard menu but 4 minutes away is must-book U Bansethů (Tâborská 389 – ubansethu.cz), a restaurant famed for its duck dishes, next to the Bašta brewery.

▶ KLÁŠTERNÍ PIVOVAR STRAHOV

🛈 🍴 Strahovské Nádvoří 301 – klasterhi-pivovar.cz – *daily 10.00-22.00 – tram 22: Pohořelec*

Contestably the best of Prague's new wave brewpubs, Sv. Norbert's 'cloister brewery' sits by the restored monastery of Strahov, high above the city, beyond the castle and Parliament. Above average food accompanies a wide range of US-Czech

U SLOVANSKÉ LÍPY

fusion beers. Come by tram from Malostranská metro then take the walk back down into town.

▶ BEER GEEK BAR
🛈 Vinohradská 62 – beergeek.cz – *daily 15.00-02.00 – metro A: Jiřího z Poděbrad*

Just opposite the Nusle exit from the metro is this modern cellar bar with 32 rotating taps, for beers from 'friends' – meaning international craft producers and a few better heritage breweries. No food and very few bottles, though their shop two blocks away, Beer Geek Pivotéka (Slavikova 10 – Su 15.00-21.00; others 12.00-21.00) sells ±500.

▶ U SLOVANSKÉ LÍPY
🛈 🍴 Tachovské Náměstí 6 – *uslovanskelipy.cz – daily 11.00-24.00 – tram 1,2, 5, 7, 9, 11, 13, 15, 26, 31: Lipanská*

Near the top of the Žižkov ridge, so also accessible via the 300-m pedestrian tunnel under Vitkov Hill from Křižíkova metro, this smart, high-ceilinged old victualling house serves traditional Bohemian food with beers from ±20 small independent Czech breweries of all eras. The owners repeat the formula almost as well in lower Žižkov at **U Vodoucha** (Jagellonská 21 – unvodoucha.cz – shut Su; Sa 12.00-23.00; Mo-Fr 11.00-23.00) and in town at U Šumavy (Štěpánská 3 – usumavy.cz – Sa-Su 12.00-23.00; Mo-Fr 11.00-23.00).

▶ LYA'S
🛈 Krymská 39 – lyabeercafe.cz – *daily 16.00-24.00 – tram 4, 13, 22: Ruská*

For the cuter end of the Prague beer scene, this hand-crafted, family-run small café and beer garden in the increasingly beery and trending Vršovice offers Lambics and other sour beers on a carefully chosen list, along with great coffee, a short list of snacks and even some cake. Wandering around the area will bring numerous other finds.

BEER GEEK BAR

▶ BASE CAMP

⊕ Muchova 241 – pifko.info – *daily 11.00-23.00 – metro A or tram 1,2, 8, 18, 20, 25, 26: Hradčanská*

If you are around for a while, or simply need a supply to drink in your lodgings, the best beer shop in Prague currently is less than 200m from Hradčanská metro. An explorer's paradise, with over 500 beers stocked from a wide range of countries and traditions. The tasting notes on line are good too, so stalk your list of purchases ahead of visiting.

Two other places to drink in the centre are rooftop **T-Anker** (Náměstí Republiky 656 – t-anker.cz – daily 11.00-22.00), above the Kotva shopping mall on the main square, an ideal spot to wait for anyone set on seeing the sights or doing some shopping without you; and Bohemian cultural anchor **U Zlatého Tygra** (Husova 17 – uzlatehotygra.cz – daily 15.00-23.00), or Golden Tiger, where tank Pilsener Urquell and lighter snacks have entertained presidents and commoners alike for over 300 years. For a decent independent take on where else to drink in Prague, try praguebeergarden.com.

NEED TO KNOW

Czech is not an easy language to master but don't let communication fears get in the way of exploring the rest of this gentle and beautiful country, which you can easily tour by staying only in brewery hotels. Much is also accessible on day-trips by train and bus, or simply by cycling alongside the Vitava river.

🛏 **Accommodation:** The castle side of the river is prettier, the town side livelier. Hotels and apartments abound, from all eras. Prices vary hugely with the season. The Old Town is pricier and less beery, so consider staying just out of the centre, in Žižkov say, near a tram or metro link. This also avoids the stag parties that swarm around Wenceslas Square at weekends.

🚌 **Getting around:** The city's simple and impressively efficient three-line metro system covers the ground fast. The citywide trams and buses connect most other places. Tickets for the whole network cost CZK30 for 30 minutes, CZK40 for 90 minutes, CZK120 for 24 hours, CZK330 for 72 hours, or CZK550 for 30 days, and are available at the airport, train and metro stations.

🍴 **Food:** While it is possible to dine elegantly in Prague, for standard fayre think mid-European stews, cuts of overcooked pork, lightly fermented cabbage, dumplings or potatoes, thick gravies, and cremated game with preserved fruits. Presentation could do better and vegetarians can still struggle. Try the pickled varieties of cheese, sausage and vegetables too.

☆ **Hints:** In contrast to the rest of the Czech Republic a tip of up to 10% is now expected in restaurants and for table service in bars. The Czech version of deadpan humour is up there with British and Flemish.

PRAGUE **131**

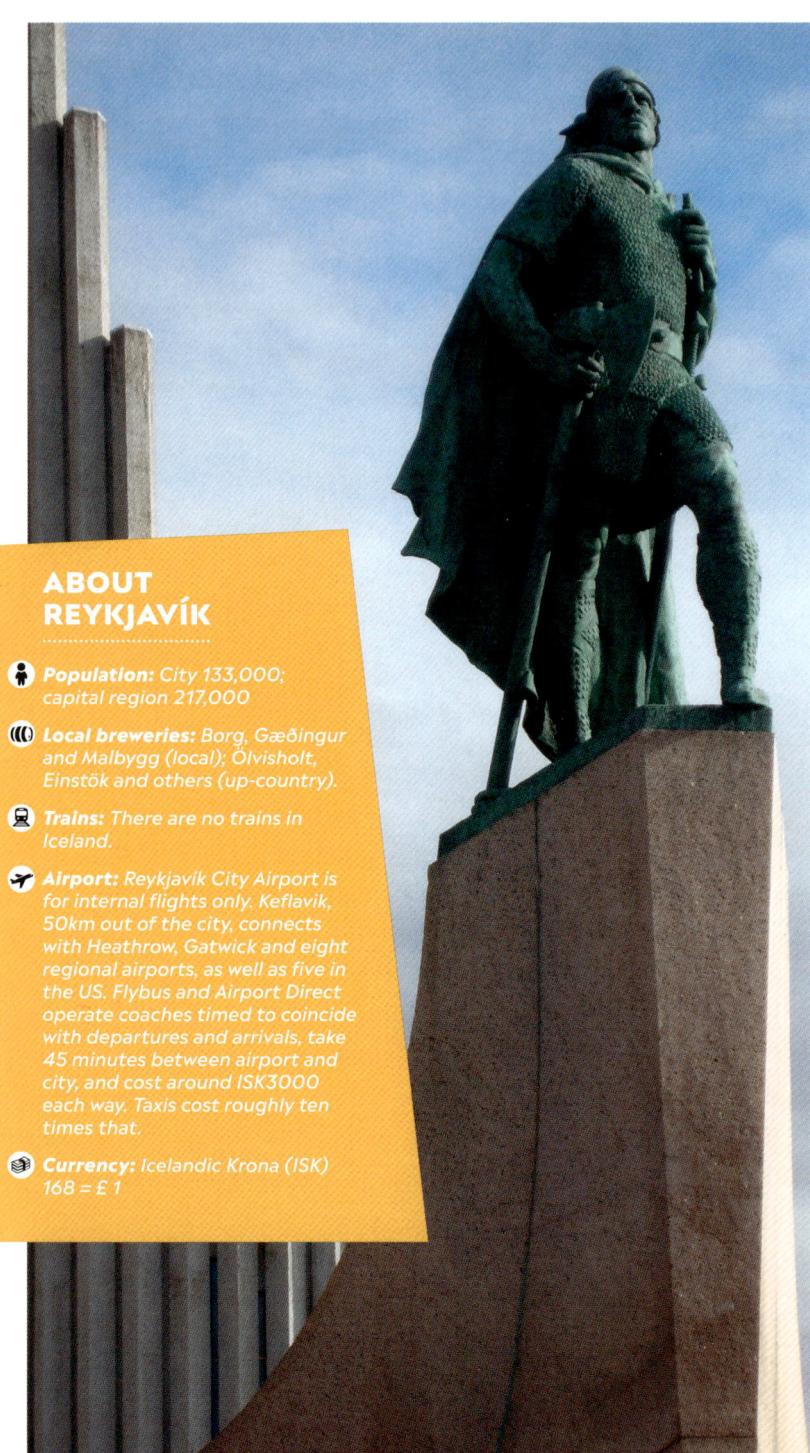

ABOUT REYKJAVÍK

- **Population:** City 133,000; capital region 217,000

- **Local breweries:** Borg, Gæðingur and Malbygg (local); Ölvisholt, Einstök and others (up-country).

- **Trains:** There are no trains in Iceland.

- **Airport:** Reykjavík City Airport is for internal flights only. Keflavík, 50km out of the city, connects with Heathrow, Gatwick and eight regional airports, as well as five in the US. Flybus and Airport Direct operate coaches timed to coincide with departures and arrivals, take 45 minutes between airport and city, and cost around ISK3000 each way. Taxis cost roughly ten times that.

- **Currency:** Icelandic Krona (ISK) 168 = £ 1

REYKJAVÍK

Anyone who can afford it should go to massive, sparsely populated Iceland and spend as much time as the schedule and bank account allow. Plan your time to include a trip out to see a geyser, the volcanic wastelands and some basalt towers at the very least.

Prohibition was imposed in Iceland in 1915 and only lifted in stages. Proper beer was the last alcoholic beverage to be legalised, on 1st March 1989, possibly because its criminalisation annoyed the Danes. Icelanders have now caught up, beer accounting for over 60% of all the alcohol sold, and smaller breweries are thriving.

Local circumstances have created a near unique situation for Europe, in that no brewery is owned, even in part, by a global corporation. The national chain of state-owned Vínbuðin off-licenses, plus a few craft beer bars, stock many better imports but at the heart of the city's beer scene are the country's two dozen or so local breweries.

The must-see attraction is Hallgrímskirkja, completed in 1986 and the country's tallest and most striking building. The nearby statue of explorer Leif Erikson, who first recorded contact with America five centuries before Columbus, was a gift from the US in 1930 to commemorate the Icelandic Parliament's first thousand years in debate.

BEER VENUES

Reykjavík is a small, compact city, built around an old harbour that is more restrained than most despite its continuing economic importance and exposure to challenging weather. The beeriest zone is a couple of blocks inland, either side of pedestrianised Laugevegur.

▶ SKÚLI

🏠 🍴 Aðalstræti 9 - FB/skulicraft – *Fr-Sa 12.00-01.00; Su-Th 12.00-23.00*

Currently the city's top craft beer bar. Dark but not gloomy, atmospheric but not kitsch, it is full of special beers, many Icelandic, as well as its large range of special brews from Borg. Ask the knowledgeable staff to guide you through whatever other Icelandic brews they have in stock. Can be delightfully quiet in the day. Enough interesting snacks to keep you there.

▶ ÍSLENSKI BARINN

🍴 Ingólfsstræti 1A - islenskibarinn.is
– *Fr-Sa 11.30-03.00; others 11.30-01.00*

Found between the centre and the foot of Laugevegur, 'The Icelandic Bar' is the city's best specialist eating house. As well as stocking a wide range of Icelandic beers and spirits, its menu includes traditional dishes like smoked lamb, reindeer, horse, puffin breast, whale fin, dung-smoked fish and aged fermented shark. Expect the exceptional.

▶ BARION BRYGGJAN BRUGGHÚS

🛈 🍴 Grandagarði 8 – barion.is – *Fr-Sa 11.30-23.00*

The first of Reykjavík's brewpubs appeared in 2015 down by the harbourside, replete in steel and copper and clearly meaning business. Up to a dozen beers appear, along with Icelandic-brewpub fusion cuisine. For a craftier equivalent try Bastard Brew & Food (Vegamótastigur 4 – bastard.is – Mo-Fr 11.30-01.00; Sa-Su 12.00-04.00), off the city end of Grettisgata.

▶ RVK BREWERY CO

🛈 Skipholt 31 – rvkbrewing.com – *shut Su-We; Thu-Sa 16.00-22.00*

The RVK taproom, for beer and vinyl, is accessed via a car lot at 174-176 Laugavegur, out near some of the cheaper hotels and apartments. If the trek looks too daunting the Bruggastofan (Snorrebraut 56 – bruggstofan.com) serves their full range of beers, along with a slow BBQ, amid studied-tatty décor.

ÍSLENSKI BARINN

MICROBAR

ÍSLENSKI BARINN

▶ VINBUÐIN AUSTURSTRÆTI

🍷 Austurstræti 10A – *shut Su; Fr 11.00-19.00; others 11.00-18.00*

For any take-home alcohol in Iceland, you need to find one of these state-owned stores. Reykjavík has eight and this is the most central. The chain now stocks over 600 beers, a quarter of which are Icelandic. If you are around for a few days, they can usually source any that are not in stock.

▶ GÆDINGUR BRUGGHÚS

🍷 Nýbýlavegur 8, Kópavogur – gaedingur.beer – *shut Mo; Tu-Su 16.00-23.00*

Árne Hafstad is not a name known or easily pronounced outside of Iceland. He owns the Gæðingur brewery and has had immense influence on his country's beer scene. This is the edge-of-town taphouse for a second Gæðingur brewhouse, included because in early 2022 the legendary **Microbar**, the top beer venue he also owns, was between lives, though as we went to press it re-opened at Laugevegur 86, in the centre. On the opposite side of the city, the other taproom worth finding is **Malbygg** (Skútuvogur 1H – malbygg.is – Th-Sa 16.00-23.00).

NEED TO KNOW

Iceland is dark and cold in winter, and beautifully lit with long days in summer. Beer Liberation Day, on 1 March each year, is preceded by a loosely arranged 'beer week'. There are bargains to be had in top-rate styles of warm clothing.

🛏 **Accommodation:** Stay as close to the centre as possible as that is where the places of most interest are found. Apartments or Airbnb properties offer best value. Prices double between June and August, when posh hotels are usually exorbitant.

🚌 **Getting around:** The city is compact and the main sites central, so walking is a viable option. There is no tram or metro system; bus routes are designed for locals, and taxis are expensive.

🍴 **Food:** Icelandic fish is a huge export commodity but Arctic char is mostly held back for local consumption and can be good value. For the rest, the skills of Iceland's chefs have been honed to justify the high prices, so try to budget for a splurge.

✴ **Hints:** It is not for a beer book to describe the theme of the Icelandic Phallological Museum (Kalkofnsvegur 2; phallus.is). Look it up if you like.

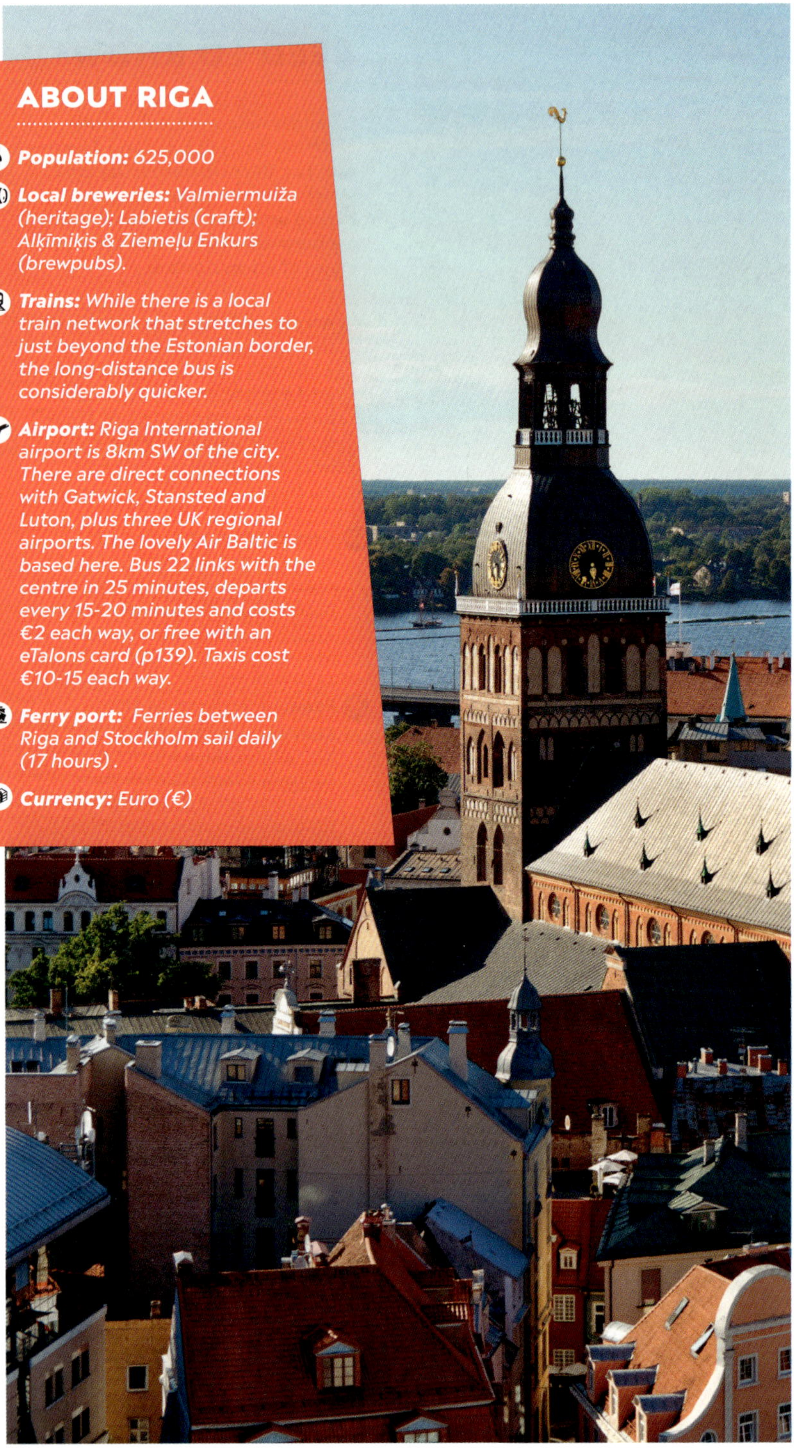

ABOUT RIGA

Population: 625,000

Local breweries: Valmiermuiža (heritage); Labietis (craft); Alķīmiķis & Ziemeļu Enkurs (brewpubs).

Trains: While there is a local train network that stretches to just beyond the Estonian border, the long-distance bus is considerably quicker.

Airport: Riga International airport is 8km SW of the city. There are direct connections with Gatwick, Stansted and Luton, plus three UK regional airports. The lovely Air Baltic is based here. Bus 22 links with the centre in 25 minutes, departs every 15-20 minutes and costs €2 each way, or free with an eTalons card (p139). Taxis cost €10-15 each way.

Ferry port: Ferries between Riga and Stockholm sail daily (17 hours).

Currency: Euro (€)

RIGA

Riga is a proper national capital, built outwards from the original Baltic sea port at the mouth of the Daugava river. The city is developing its own take on modern Euroculture – part Scandi hipster, part Polish work ethic. In its Old Town, made up of confused streets spraying out from the Freedom Monument, the challenge is to spot the bits of Imperial Russian, Soviet, Nordic and Euro architecture that define its identity issues.

In the days of the Russian Czars, Latvia was a large producer of Stouts and Porters, but between 1915 and the death of Stalin in 1953 it lost all but two breweries. A small network of partially state-owned, local lager breweries began to appear by the time of independence from Russia in 1993, since when efforts to modernise the beer scene have spluttered and popped.

The regional talent remains for uncompromising Stouts, though folk brews with added honey and local herbs appear, and all things sour and fruity are trending. However, if you can taste past the gratuitous haze, there is hop wizardry in some Latvian Pale Ales, while a few of the golden (gaišais) and dark (tumšais) heritage lagers are classy.

Whatever else you do while in town, take in as much as you can tolerate of the Central Market, immediately south of the main station. UNESCO-protected, it is an early example of urban renewal. Its five pavilions, built as Zeppelin airship hangars in the First World War, now house over 3,000 small stands and shops.

BEER VENUES

Expect every type of bar in Riga. Stag parties tend to slick along Livu Square in the Old Town, their plastic devoured by sellers of predictable pleasures. The beerier quarters are centred in the area between the Central Market and the Uzvaras Boulevard bridge to the south of the centre, and along a spur that follows tram route 11.

▶ ARMOURY BAR

🛈 🍴 Vecpilsētas iela 11 – the-armoury-bar.business.site – *daily 16.00-23.00 – tram 5: 13th Janvāra iela*

A great little bar in the back alleys of Old Riga, 100m as the crow flies or 400m on foot from the next entry. Specialises in craft beers and better whiskies from around the world, presented in a cosy, granite-walled bar, taking its name from the impressive collection of armaments, including machine guns and grenades, that adorn its walls.

ALUS CELLE

▶ MIEZIS & KOMPĀNIJA

🛈 13 Janvāra iela 21 – FB/miezisvecriga – daily 14.00-02.00 – tram 5: 13th Janvāra iela

Odd but excellent beer bar under the Avalon Hotel. This chic warehouse-like space, kitted out with thick hardwoods, concrete, tall wooden stools and plywood lampshades, is so far beyond Soviet that it almost meets it coming back. The beer selection is a long, picky list of European greats at affordable prices, plus Latvian hopefuls, displayed by size and style. Ethnic nibbles only.

▶ BEERA BAR

🛈🍴 Ģertrūdes iela 39 – beerabar.lv – Sa-Su 14.00-23.00; Mo-Fr 15.00-23.00 – tram 1, 11: Ģertrūdes iela

COVID saw beer bars in Latvia suffer, to the benefit of those that also operated a beer shop. So it was that this specialist bar, which tries to source beers from wherever, swapped its model to takeaway for the duration of the pandemic. Awash with flavoured ales but stocking some good and unusual grown-up ones too. No food.

▶ TAKA

🛈🍴 Miera 10 – FB/takabars – Su 18.00-24.00; Mo-Sa 16.00-24.00 – tram 11: Brīvības iela

This individual beer bar is far enough from the centre for the local housing to be wooden. Its list of 80 local and imported beers is supported by light home-cooked snacks. Two blocks further out and one block to the left, on Aristida Biana iela, are the back-to-back but very different taphouses for the Labietis (daily from 15.00) and Valmiermuiža (daily from 10.00) breweries.

▶ ALUS CELLE

🛈🍴 Baznīcas iela 35 – aluscelle.lv – Su 12.00-20.00; others 12.00-22.00 – tram 11: Brīvības iela

The owner of the 'Beer Cellar' is one of the people who helped to bring better beer to Latvia from all over the world. The shop remains the larger part of the business and ships to all of Europe. Its cosy cave of a tasting room lends itself to beer chat, and it has a small, streetside terrace. No food, but the Tex-Mex on the corner has local beers.

▸ BEERFOX

🛈 🕒 **Stabu iela 59** – *shut Su; Mo-We 11.00-21.00; Th-Sa 11.00-22.00* – *trolley 22: Stabu iela*

Another place that gave the Latvian beer scene a good shake is this beer shop run by a half-hippy/half-entrepreneur Nebraskan, designed to bring Latvians the best of (mainly northern) European beer. It has now added an eponymous beer bar next door (Su 16.00-23.00; others from 12.00). The local range is limited but the rest is world class.

LABIETIS

NEED TO KNOW

Latvians speak to Lithuanians in English, because it is the compulsory second language in each country's schools. That said, the English-speaking tourist still needs an ear for what different accents do to vowel sounds and consonants.

🛏 **Accommodation:** Hotels and apartments abound at roughly half the European normal price. The attractions are mostly on the east bank of the Daugava river, though there are some excellent places to stay just over the bridges on the west bank.

🚌 **Getting around:** The buses, trams and trolley buses share ticketing but urban trains do not. There are two types of eTalons (eTicket). A yellow cardboard one is for loading 24-hour (€5), 3- (€10) or 5-day (€15) passes, while a blue plastic one is for loading up to 50 trips at €1.15 each, dropping to ±€1 each after the first 10. Bolt is here; Uber is not.

🍴 **Food:** Latvian cuisine is not really a thing, though there are Latvian ingredients, such as pickled vegetables, dumplings, grey peas and dark rye bread. The last of these features in a dark, sweet comfort pudding called maizes zupa. Rasol is a thick potato, vegetable and egg salad, typically layered with saltfish or cured meat.

⭐ **Hints:** Tip up to 10% in cash at restaurants and 50 cents in other settings. Riga Black Balsam, a vodka-based herbal liqueur, should be tasted before bringing any home for a cherished or vulnerable relative.

ABOUT ROME

- **Population:** City 2,350,000; metropolitan area 4,390,000
- **Local breweries:** Ritual Lab and Rebel's (craft).
- **Trains:** Termini, Rome's main station, is in the central area and has direct connections with Bologna (<100 a day; 2.0-2.5 hours).
- **Ferry port:** Ferries between Civitavecchia, 40km NW of Rome, and Barcelona (20 hours) sail a couple of times a week.
- **Airport:** Classy Fiumicino airport is on the coast 30km SW of the city and has direct connections with Heathrow, Gatwick, Luton and eight regional UK airports. The Leonardo Express links to Termini station every 15 minutes, takes 32 minutes and costs €14 each way, or €40 for a group of 4. The equally frequent FL1 train links to Tiburtina station in 48 minutes and costs €8, while taxis cost €50-60. Functional Ciampino airport has direct connections with most London airports, Manchester and Edinburgh, and connects with the city via a combined bus and train service that links to Termini in 30-40 minutes and costs €2.70 each way.
- **Currency:** Euro (€)

ROME

The story of European beer's journey back to better began with traditional beer nations growing swathes of new brewers to replace those lost in the 20th century. Then came Italy, carving out a new type of beer culture, for which there was no historic precedent. With over 1000 operating breweries and several hundred beer companies that commission own-label beers, Italian brewing has never been healthier. Nowhere is this more obvious than in the capital, Rome.

The city's other tourist attractions can be grouped into pre-Christian (the Colosseum, Forum, Pantheon, Catacombs and Palatine Hill); Christian (the Vatican, the Basilica of St. John Lateran, and the church of Santa Maria Maggiore); and romantic (the Spanish Steps, Trevi Fountain, Piazza Navona, and Villa Borghese).

Be warned, however, that all these attract lengthy queues, with crowds squeezed like pizza dough, non-stop in summer and for much of the day at other times.

Those who go into raptures about Rome have in mind intimate restaurants and laid-back bars in backstreet neighbourhoods. So might you. Snap the best from a hop-on hop-off bus tour or, if you don't mind looking stupid, the 3-hour Rome Segway Tour.

BEER DESTINATIONS

Most people asked to name an Italian beer would likely pick Peroni or Moretti, the cold pasta brands of Italian lager. Birra artigianale, or Italian craft beer, has nothing in common with these industrial lightweights, as you will see in the capital's many types of beer bar, the best of which sit, by pure coincidence, just off the route of tram 8.

▶ MA CHE SIETE VENUTI A FÀ
ⓘ Via Benedetta 25 - football-pub.com – daily 11.00-02.00 – tram 8: Belli

Off the west bank of the Tiber near Sisto bridge, the name of the original Roman beer bar translates roughly as 'Why Have You Come Here'. Though it bills itself as a football pub this is a simple, cosy altar to great beer in all formats, on a list of 100+ bottles and cans, 16 taps, plus a couple of handpulls to serve Italian ales at UK carbonation level.

▶ L'ELEMENTARE TRAVASTERE
ⓘ 🍴 Via Benedetta 23 - FB/elementaretravastere – Fr from 16.00; Sa from 12.00; Su-Th from 17.00 – tram 8: Belli

When the former Bir & Fud, a few metres up the way from the last entry, morphed into L'Elementare in 2018, I think that nothing major changed so expect a pleasant pizzeria with a well-balanced menu of Italian beers and imports, a dozen on tap and 100+ in bottle. If the beef tartare with dried tomato and grain mustard survived, try it.

▶ OPEN BALADIN

🛈 🍴 Via degli Specchi 6 – baladin.it – *daily from 12.00 – tram 8: Arenula*

Teo Musso's ground-breaking Baladin brewery was founded in 1986 and this high-ceilinged, orange cavern is its temple in the capital, with 38 taps and 80+ bottles from all over. Try a small glass of their Xyauyù, the beer equivalent of vintage port, at a not dissimilar price. There is a broad range of pastas, burgers, salads and sandwiches.

▶ LUPPULO STATION

🛈 🍴 Via Giuseppe Parini 4 – luppulostation.com – *Su from 12.00; Mo-Sa from 17.00 – tram 3, 8: Trastevere Pascarelle*

Near to Trastevere train station, which has two slow trains an hour to Termini, this appealing place is too large to be a den and too well-furnished to be a dive. There is much leather seating, plus lots of helpful servers to guide you through its 20 taps and larger bottled list. Burgers, tacos and Italian fast food, with better specials.

▶ LES VIGNERONS

🔒 S Via Goffredo Mamili 61 – lesvignerons.it – *shut Su; Mo 16.00-20.30; Tu-Fr 11.00-20.30 – tram 8: Min Istruzione*

This delightful wine shop, just off

OPEN BALADIN

Trastevere, carries not so much a beer range as a bespoke collection of handpicked beers from around Europe, plus the sort of knowledge about its stock that all great shops should possess. A place to buy some specials to take home rather than supplying a party.

▶ MAD FOR BEER

🛈 🍴 Via Federico Ozanam 62 – madforbeerpub.com – *daily 16.00-02.00* – *tram 8: San Giovanni di Dio*

This self-styled pub specialises in British and American beers, with some Italian, Czech and others appearing. Ten taps and a bottled list of 30+ are sometimes supplemented with oysters, though most of the food, in line with the place itself, is more UK-Italian fusion pub menu. At the southern end of the tram 8 run.

NEED TO KNOW

It will take some time before Italian brewing is acclaimed as much as the country's wine, though the notion that it might be is no longer fanciful, not least for the exorbitant prices charged nowadays for some of the latter.

🛏 **Accommodation:** Hotels and apartments abound all over the city. Termini station is the main transport hub, and staying out of the centre, a short walk from a metro station – or the tram 8 line – can save considerably, particularly in summer.

🚇 **Getting around:** There are 3.5 metro lines, 6 principal tram routes, countless buses and some confusing local trains but all bar the Leonardo Express are covered by the same tickets. A single journey (<100 minutes) costs €1.50; a day-long ticket (to 24.00) €7; 2-day €12.50; 3-day €18; and 7-day €24, from metro stations, tobacconists, plus some bars and bus stops.

🍴 **Food:** Eating well is easy, at a price. However, for more basic local specialities try allesso di bollito, a primitive form of burger; cacio e pepe (pecorino cheese and black pepper) or else the local cream-free carbonara on pasta; suppli (rice croquettes with chopped meat); a hot porchetta pork sandwich or traditional trippa (tripe).

☆ **Hints:** Tipping means topping up. Expect many hotels and restaurants to carry a few local beers. Drinking in Italy is strictly a social pursuit and not for getting drunk.

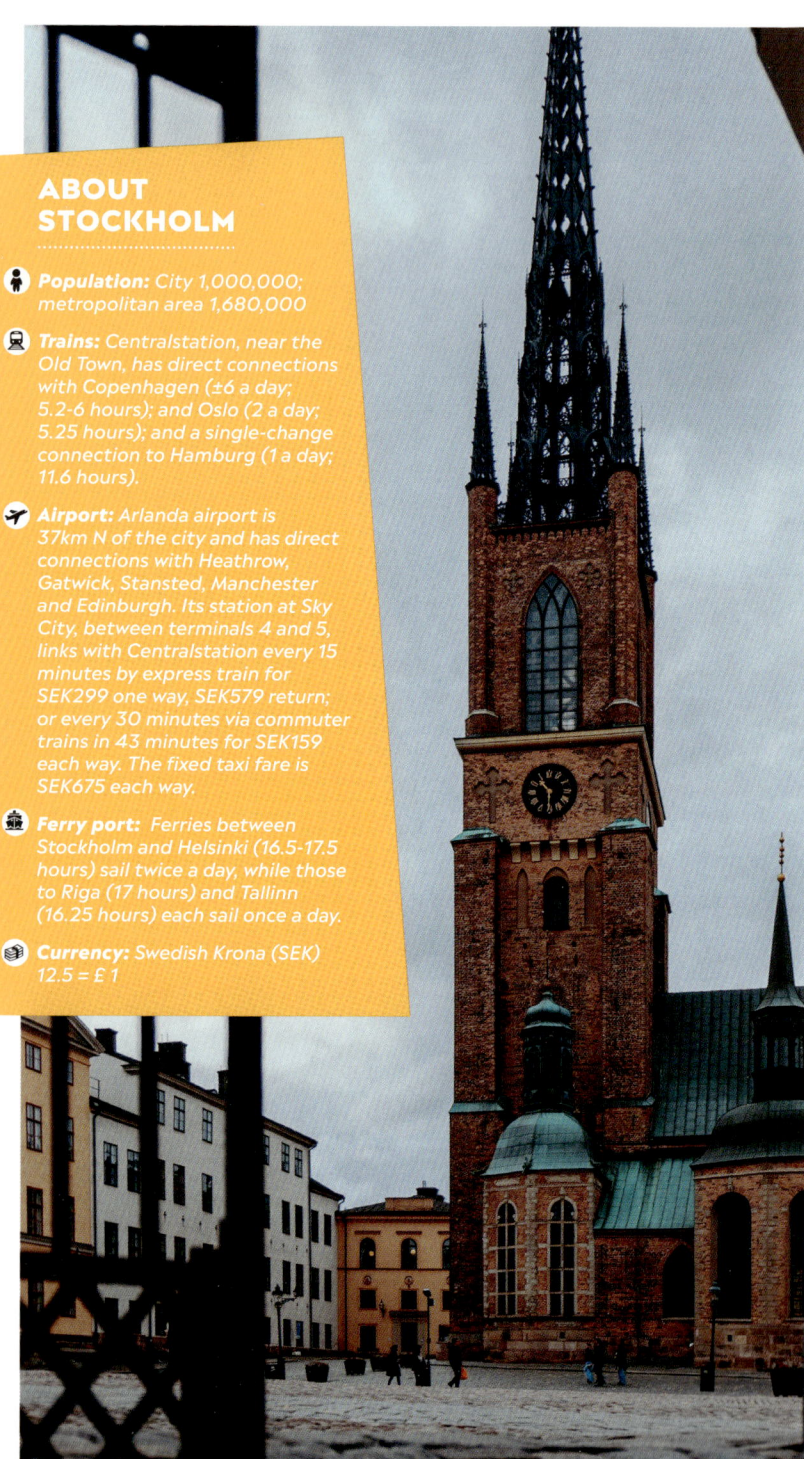

ABOUT STOCKHOLM

Population: City 1,000,000; metropolitan area 1,680,000

Trains: Centralstation, near the Old Town, has direct connections with Copenhagen (±6 a day; 5.2-6 hours); and Oslo (2 a day; 5.25 hours); and a single-change connection to Hamburg (1 a day; 11.6 hours).

Airport: Arlanda airport is 37km N of the city and has direct connections with Heathrow, Gatwick, Stansted, Manchester and Edinburgh. Its station at Sky City, between terminals 4 and 5, links with Centralstation every 15 minutes by express train for SEK299 one way, SEK579 return; or every 30 minutes via commuter trains in 43 minutes for SEK159 each way. The fixed taxi fare is SEK675 each way.

Ferry port: Ferries between Stockholm and Helsinki (16.5-17.5 hours) sail twice a day, while those to Riga (17 hours) and Tallinn (16.25 hours) each sail once a day.

Currency: Swedish Krona (SEK) 12.5 = £ 1

STOCKHOLM

The Swedish capital is built on a 14-island archipelago linked by fifty bridges and numerous ferries. To appreciate its full splendour, take at least one long ferry ride along the fjord, perhaps to Skansen Open Air Museum (the world's first in 1891) or, if nothing else can save you, the Abba Museum. Take in too the Royal Palace and distinctive cobbled streets of the Old Town (Gamla Stan).

There is no dodging the fact that Sweden is expensive, with Stockholm more so, which includes its beer. The Swedes pay a lot of tax and expect a lot for it. The tax on alcohol is high but pathologically fair, being in direct proportion to the amount of alcohol in the drink. For take-home, drinks above 3.5% ABV can only be bought from the state-run chain of Systembolaget shops.

The Swedish beer scene, which now boasts 300+ breweries making all types of beer, has blossomed in recent decades. This has been assisted by beer brand advertising being banned, and further by Systembolaget allowing new brewers access to their local stores, with the best gaining national distribution.

BEER VENUES

The Swedes drink 80% of their beer at home, a fact reflected in the relative lack of bars and pubs, most of which serve food. Three-quarters of Stockholm's 'breweries', most prominently Omnipollo, are marketing operations that do little or no brewing themselves, though you may not see that on the labels.

▶ AKKURAT

ℹ️ 🍴 BF Hornsgatan 18 – akkurat.se
– Fr-Su from 13.00; Mo-Th from 15.00 –
metro / bus: Slussen

To understand this awesome place, you need to visit several times. Near to the Slussen transport hub and 500m from the quay, this is one of the world's top beer bars. Its huge beer offer, and whisky list, illustrate every style and origin, and the

ever-better menu is developing to match this. Pre-COVID, closing time at this bucket list destination was around 01.00.

▶ OLIVER TWIST

🛈🍴 Repslagargatan 6 – olivertwist.se
– *Sa-Su from 12.00; Mo-Fr from 11.00; high summer from 16.00 daily – metro / bus: Slussen*

This well-designed, well-kept and lovable pub would be the top beer bar in any other city. Equally close to Slussen but two blocks south of the last entry, it stocks over 200 Swedish, US and UK beers, with up to 30 on draught, including a couple of cask ales. The food is designed to sustain nicely rather than impress. The spade to Akkurat's bucket.

▶ MAN IN THE MOON

🛈🍴 Tegnérgatan 2C – maninthemoon.se – *shut Su; Sa 12.00-01.00; others from 11.00 – metro: Rådmansgatan, or bus 2, 96: Tegnérgatan*

This hefty pub-restaurant to the north of the centre is more must-try than bucket list. The ambience would pass for Edwardian British or solid German. Its beer offer is split between those commissioned from top Scandinavian producers, 30 taps and an impressive list of aged bottles. The prominent food menu includes Elk Bourgignon.

▶ INTERNATIONELLA PRESSKLUBBEN

🍴 Vasagatan 50 – pressklubben.se
– *shut Su; Sa 16.00-24.00; Mo-Fr 11.00-24.00 – Centralstation / T-Centralen*

If you are on a budget, pass by. The Press Club is an elegant restaurant aimed at people who have a refined palate and a serious love of Belgian beer. This is where you take a beer-loving client, or hope you are taken to by someone who really likes you. The world-beating beer list is almost entirely Belgian, reaching 800, from 150 breweries.

▶ ZUM FRANZISKANER

🛈🍴 Skeppsbron 44 – zumen.se
– *Fr-Su from 15.00; Mo-Th from 16.00 – metro: Gamla Stan & Slussen, or bus / tram station: Kornhamnstorg*

Run since 2018 by the long-serving former manager of Akkurat, this handsome looking old beer hall of German-Swedish design, near to Slussen Quay, makes a neat triangle

with Akkurat and Oliver Twist (above). Made up of two halves, it has a bar with a highly imaginative beer list and a restaurant serving a proper menu of Swedish dishes.

▶ SYSTEMBOLAGET PK HUSET

🚪 Norrlandgatan 3 - Systembolaget.se
– shut Su; Sa 10.00-15.00; others 10.00-19.00 – tram 7: Kungsträdgården

Among the largest of Sweden's ±450 Systembolaget shops, found in the basement of a department store. The block also houses the HQ of Nordea Bank. This one routinely stocks around 2,000 beers, including hundreds from small Swedish breweries, though like all branches they can order in any of the chain's list of ±3,300. Age limit 20.

MAN IN THE MOON

NEED TO KNOW

Stockholm can be cold and gloomy from mid-December to mid-March but makes up for it from the end of May to the end of September. Be aware though that the high summer exodus can see some businesses close. To keep costs down, buy in brunch from a supermarket, drink stronger beers in smaller measures and maximise your use of public transport.

🛏 **Accommodation:** Prices vary enormously with the season, location and what's on in town, though expensive is the average. Airbnb etc come into their own in summer, the excellent transport links enabling a stay in the suburbs.

🚌 **Getting around:** The bus, tram, metro (Tunnelbana), urban train and local ferry network is co-ordinated by Storstockholms Lokaltrafik (sl.se). Ticketing is moving swiftly toward contactless SL Card only. Single tickets valid for 75 minutes cost SEK39 (or SEK54 on the spot); 24 hours is SEK165, 72 hours SEK330, 7 days SEK430 or 30 days SEK970.

🍴 **Food:** If your food rules allow, you should enjoy fish in the form of gravlax (cured salmon), numerous types of pickled herring, crayfish, skagen toast (shrimp in sauce) and the local fish pie, Janssons frestelse. More for bulk are meatballs in a gravy sometimes enlivened by lingonberry jam.

⭐ **Hints:** Tips are not expected, except on things like the 'free' walking tours of the Gamla Stan. English is spoken everywhere. Bits of the metro are a free art gallery and some ferries make a great city tour.

ABOUT TALLINN

Population: 450,000

Local breweries: Põhjala, Õllenaut, Tanker, Sori, Pühaste, Vormsi & Lehe (Estonian).

Trains: While there is a local train network, with a few meeting Latvian trains at the border, the long-distance bus is considerably quicker.

Airport: Tallinn airport is 4km SW of the city and has direct connections with Gatwick, Stansted, Edinburgh and Liverpool. Tram 4 and Bus 2 make regular departures for the centre, cost €2 each way or are included on a regular travel card. Taxis cost ±€12 each way.

Ferry port: Ferries sail between Tallinn and Helsinki (2.5-3 hours) up to 8 times a day; and Stockholm (16.5 hours) once a day.

Currency: Euro (€)

TALLINN

I love Tallinn, the more so since the stag parties were largely seen off by selective licensing. Its Old Town, with its unique mix of northern, eastern and central European elements, reeks of history. The language is even more challenging than Finnish.

When I first visited in 2010, better beer was confined to some big-tasting legacy Porters and Stouts from three large industrial producers, a few halfway decent darker lagers from a small brewery up-country, and the so-so beers from a single German-style Hausbrauerei. Koduõlu, a farmhouse ale similar to Sahti, made on the island of Saaremaa, was unobtainable, as were most imports.

Twelve years on, Estonia is one of the most confident brewing nations in Europe, its fifty or so new producers being obliged by their role model, Põhjala, to keep high standards, though imports now abound, making them aware of the competition. While some beers contain odd fruits, odder yeasts, or spruce tips, it is the classic styles of Porter-Stout and paler ales at which Estonian brewing excels.

For history, meander through the mostly uncrowded streets of the Old Town and stare at the buildings. Then put it in proportion by climbing the narrow, cobbled streets to the Kohtuotsa viewing platform on the north side of Toompea Hill. For something more contemporary find Telliskivi Creative City.

BEER VENUES

Young Estonians like beer and while bar owners are not afraid to ask €4.50 for a bottle of something decent, there is often little price difference between a session Pale Ale and an Imperial Stout. The venues below are either in the narrow streets of the Old Town, surrounded but not served by public transport, or else somewhere near the 73 bus route.

▶ KOHT

🛈🍴 8 Lai - FB/tubakas - *daily from 17.00*

The 'Tavern' is snuck behind a beer shop called Õllepood, or 'Pothouse' (daily 10.00-22.00), which between them make the city's best beer destination. For arcane licensing reasons they are separate businesses, so take-home beer must be bought in the shop and may not be drunk in the cosy bar or on its enclosed terrace. The furnishings are equally unsynchronised.

▶ PÕRGU

🛈🍴 4 Rüütli - porgu.ee – *shut Su; Mo-Th 12.00-24.00; Fr-Sa 12.00-02.00*

This marvellous cellar bar, dominated by heavy wood and cast iron, becomes foody in the evening, though the kitchen closes at 22.00. Check if a reservation will be required for those times, and reserve – the food is authentic and above average. This is the most likely place to find koduõlu, as well as kali, the local form of kvass, within a wide range of beers on tap and in the bottle.

▶ UBA JA HAMAL
🏠🍺 Võrgu 3 – FB/ubajahama
Fr-Sa 12.00-23.00; Su-Th 14.00-22.00 – bus 73: Kalarand

The 'Bean & Hop' is a beer and coffee shop with a taproom, just off the route from the Old Town to the next entry. Reflecting the youthful nature of the new Estonian beer scene, it has 20 taps, lots of beers with stuff added, branded growlers for takeaway and a beer focus that makes everything forgivable. Wines and spirits too but no food.

▶ PÕHJALA BREWERY & TAP ROOM
🏠🍺 Peetri 5 – pohjalabeer.com
shut Mo; Su 10.00-17.00; Fr-Sa 12.00-02.00; others 12.00-24.00 – bus 73: Noblessneri, or 3: Volta

When Põhjala, the country's leading small, independent brewery, expanded its brewhouse into a disused factory at the old Noblessner shipyard, a high-ceilinged taphouse soon followed. The beer range stretches to 70 when collabs and celebrity beers, are included. Food is 'BBQ'. Take a taxi, or bus 73 from the previous or next entries.

▶ DRINK BAR & GRILL
🏠🍺 Väika Karja 8 – FB/Drinkbaarandgrill
Fr-Sa 12.00-02.00; Su-Th 12.00-23.00 – tram 3, 4, or bus 73: Viru

Tallinn's original and ground-breaking beer bar was created by an ex-pat Brit and still feels like a London street-corner long bar in some ways. A change of hands has brought more emphasis on late 20th century pub grub but a fairly strong list of bottled and canned Estonian beers remains, alongside more mainstream stuff on tap.

▶ HELL HUNT
🏠🍺 Pikk 39 – hellhunt.ee
daily 12.00-02.00

Another of the early adopters of new imported and home-grown beer, in the northern part of the Old Town. Part sports bar, part old-fashioned boozer, it is popular

PÕHJALA BREWERY & TAP ROOM

with younger locals for its wide range of special beers, increasingly featuring craft lookalikes, plus a typical menu of modern pub grub. Heaves and gets noisy on weekend nights.

HELL HUNT

NEED TO KNOW

While it shares common goals with the other Baltic States, Latvia and Lithuania, and is hugely respectful of its Russian neighbours, Estonia's aspirations are more clearly Nordic. In its capital this is starting to be reflected in prices, though these still have a long way to go before they catch up with Helsinki.

Accommodation: Aim for the Old Town, which remains affordable and is great to wander round at night. Summer prices, though high, remain below the European average.

Getting around: In four trips to Tallinn, I have yet to use a bus or trolley, and have only twice hopped on a tram. Walking is both viable and interesting, and registered taxis are abundant and cheap. If you need to board anything, pay the driver €2, or buy a Ühiskaart (Smartcard) from a kiosk for €2, loading it with 1-hour journeys of €1.50 each, or else for 1 (€4.50), 2 (€7.50) or 5 days (€9). No more than three journeys a day will be charged.

Food: There are remarkably few chain restaurants in the city and it is noticeable that they are not missed. Food remains fresh and quite seasonal. National favourites include smoked fish with egg on rye bread, plus the whole pork, duck and cabbage thing. The curious must try lamprey, though possibly just the once.

Hints: Tipping in restaurants must be cash. 10% is generous. Consider visiting in snowbound December for the Christmas market.

TALLINN 151

ABOUT TEL AVIV

- **Population:** City 430,000; metropolitan area 4,350,000
- **Local breweries:** Dancing Camel and Schnitt (brewpubs).
- **Airport:** Tel Aviv Ben Gurion airport is 10km SE of the centre and has direct connections with Heathrow, Luton and Manchester. The train link with Tel Aviv Ha'Hagana station and transport hub is suspended for electrification but there are buses. Taxis cost roughly ILS 150-200 each way.
- **Currency:** Israeli New Shekel (ILS) 4.34 = £ 1

TEL AVIV

I can hear your face. Surely Israel is not in Europe? Is he ignorant, or what? Maybe the Eurovision Song Contest warped his brain? Perhaps that's its purpose?

In many things, Israel is other. Not part of Asia, in but not of the Middle East, American and Russian influenced at every level, looking to Europe but not European. Tel Aviv was its Mediterranean city resort, now amalgamated with the ancient port city of Jaffa, or Yafo in Hebrew, to form Tel Aviv-Yafo, the country's economic hub, building skyscrapers for tomorrow, whenever and whatever that will be.

The real reason I included it here is that in contrast to anywhere else in the historic Middle East, modern West Asia or even North Africa, the beer scene in Israel is trying hard to be First World. Around 30 real breweries and as many pretend ones are making recognisable craft beers, some remarkably well.

Brewing is not easy here. Israel grows wheat but not brewers' barley, has no maltings, hop farms or commercial yeast banks, and its water quality can change in the course of a single brew run. Also, the government is unsympathetic to brewing, partly for politico-religious reasons and partly for the country's craft beer diaspora being from a suppressed generation. 'There are two large, disenfranchised groups in Israel today,' one brewer told me, 'The Palestinians and the under 40s.'

Hebrew is an incomprehensible scribble to the European eye, written from right to left. While many Israelis speak American, others were Russian-born and refuse.

BEER VENUES

Even in hip Tel Aviv there is no long tradition of going out with mates for a beer, so even the best beer bars are either quirky or a bit restrained. Pride in Israeli brewing has been slow to grow, though now it is, the envelope is being pushed.

▶ DANCING CAMEL

🛈 Ha-Ta'asiya Street 12 – dancingcamel.com – *shut Sa; Fr 12.00-17.00; Mo-Th 17.00-24.00*

The place that started the Israeli beer revival began brewing and serving beer in a disused 1930s granary in 2005, which is 'just down the street' from a 5,000-year-old Egyptian brewery. Entertainment includes karaoke, stand-up comedy, or live Blues. A dozen beers are brewed on the premises, with around eight usually on tap. Small snacks only.

▶ PORTER & SONS

🛈 Ha-Arba'a Street 14 – porter.co.il – *Su-We 17.00-24.00; Th-Fr 17.00-01.00; Sa 12.00-24.00*

Tel Aviv's most impressive beer venue is this distinctly European, dark wood and comfortable eating house with a long row of stools at the bar. The 50 draught beers are cared for precisely, with the 70 bottled beers adding variety that features Belgian and Israeli, with some British, Czech and US brands. The above average cooking is eastern Mediterranean with dabs of MittelEurop. Next door to Schnitt (below).

▶ BEER BAZAAR

ⓘ The Beer Bazaar chain of bars *(beerbazaar.co.il)* began with **Yishkon** *(Yishkon Street 36 – Fr from 11.00; Sa from 19.00; Su-Th from 12.00)*, just off the bustle of the Ha'Carmel food, drink and schmutter market in Tel Aviv, and recently added **Jaffa** *(Olei Zion 7, Yafo)*, with similar hours in Yafo's flea market. It also hosts pop-up bars such as **Habima** *(Rothschild Boulevard 142 – summer only: Fr 13.00-01.30; others 17.00–01.30)*.

BEER BREAKS

BEER BAZAAR

NEED TO KNOW

Israel has a habit of shutting down fairly frequently, not least for Shabbat (the Sabbath), which starts just before sundown on Friday and continues until Saturday evening, with some things not restarting until Sunday morning. Passover is a 9-day shutdown of similar intensity, akin in timing but not tradition to Easter. This is soon followed by Yom HaShoah (Holocaust Remembrance Day), a 24-hour lockdown, with a siren at 10.00 that prompts a shudder, and two minutes of resolute silence with bowed heads.

Accommodation: Hotels are surprisingly expensive, especially along the waterfront. Apartments are better bets. Aim for areas within 800m of Habima Square.

Getting around: Well, the taxis are fairly cheap, which is a good thing as there are no trams or metro and the urban trains are normally only good for the airport and currently not even that. Buses are run by four different companies, with locals in mind, not visitors.

Food: Although much is made of the kosher way of preparing food, it is not a cuisine so much as an elaborate system of etiquette such that, for example, brewpubs cannot serve milk with coffee. Food in Israel has strong similarities with other Eastern Mediterranean countries – falafels and tabbouleh, hummus and baba ganoush, flat breads and grilled meats, and olives with light white cheese in the salads. For breakfast try shakshuka – eggs baked in spicy tomato.

Hints: Tipping is 10-15% depending on effort. The palpable, low-level paranoia that pervades daily life is part history, part habit.

Pre-COVID these served ±70 Israeli beers, plus those from Taybeh in Palestine. Food typically involves a close relationship with a nearby restaurant.

▶ THE BEER SHOP

Yiehuda Ha-Levi Street 21 - beershop.co.il - Sa 16.00-01.30; Su-Fr 12.00-01.30

Despite the name, this is a beer bar dedicated to serving 30 draught beers, typically half of which are Israeli, half European, plus a smallish menu of fairly simple eats. For most of the year, the bulk of the drinking happens on its streetside terrace, though there is standing room inside and there are times when it is bar service only. Big on takeaway beer too.

▶ BEER & BEYOND

Yigal Alon St 159 - beerandbeyond.com – shut Sa; Fr 09.00-15.00; others 09.00-19.00 (Th 21.00) - train: Hashalom

Shachar Hertz is one of the drivers behind much in the Israeli beer world and his shop is where the best comes together. Carrying around 400 beers, with up to 100 Israeli, this is the country's best beer store, as well as a home brewers' emporium, some decent schwag, and more knowledge about the national brewing scene than anywhere else.

The new arrival is Schnitt (Ha-Arba'a Street 12 – schnitt.co.il – daily. 12.00-24.00), a brewpub and eating house next door to Porter & Sons, aiming to bring a local take on the urban taphouse and kitchen to the heart of the city.

TEL AVIV 155

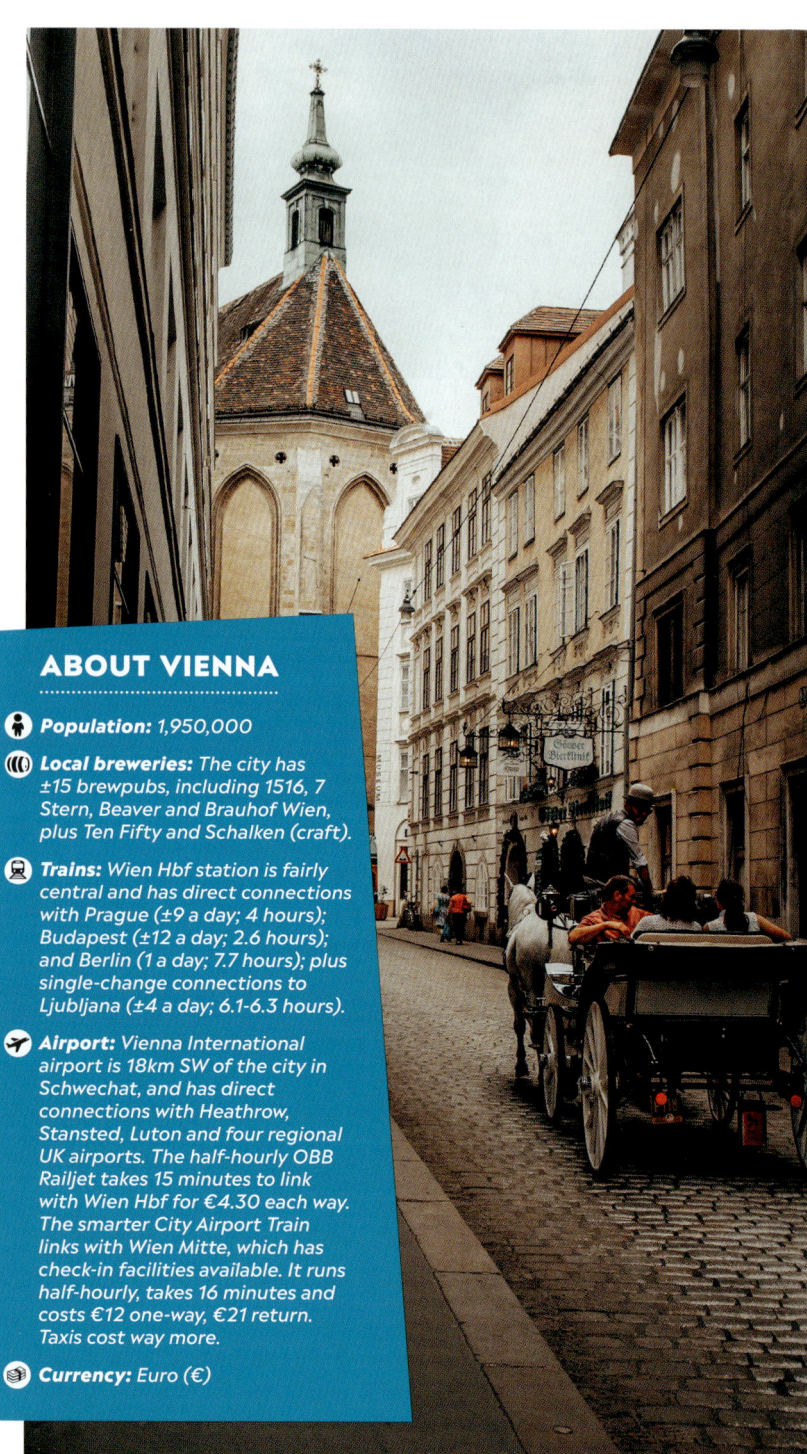

ABOUT VIENNA

Population: 1,950,000

Local breweries: The city has ±15 brewpubs, including 1516, 7 Stern, Beaver and Brauhof Wien, plus Ten Fifty and Schalken (craft).

Trains: Wien Hbf station is fairly central and has direct connections with Prague (±9 a day; 4 hours); Budapest (±12 a day; 2.6 hours); and Berlin (1 a day; 7.7 hours); plus single-change connections to Ljubljana (±4 a day; 6.1-6.3 hours).

Airport: Vienna International airport is 18km SW of the city in Schwechat, and has direct connections with Heathrow, Stansted, Luton and four regional UK airports. The half-hourly OBB Railjet takes 15 minutes to link with Wien Hbf for €4.30 each way. The smarter City Airport Train links with Wien Mitte, which has check-in facilities available. It runs half-hourly, takes 16 minutes and costs €12 one-way, €21 return. Taxis cost way more.

Currency: Euro (€)

VIENNA

The First World War saw the Austro-Hungarian Empire finally implode and left Austria bankrupt. The Second left Vienna (Wien) with extensive bomb damage, an Opera House, a clutch of palaces, and a location, on the banks of the river Danube (Donau), uncomfortably close to the 'Iron Curtain', the political border that divided Europe for the next 45 years.

Brewing pioneer Anton Dreher made one of the first commercially viable lagers in his brewery at Schwechat in 1841, though history gave more plaudits to Pilsen and Munich. The brewery is now owned by Heineken, which bought a cluster of regional breweries in 2003 and, uniquely, kept nine of them operational. Its Zipfer brewery makes a classic Austrian Märzen, softer and lighter than the German version, while at Schwechater they have revived Dreher's original ruddy-brown Vienna lager.

For the twenty or so other heritage breweries and 240+ newer ones the challenge is to market newer styles of beer to conservative drinkers raised on clarity and purity.

For tourism, focus on anything that celebrates the unparalleled musical heritage of a city that was home to Beethoven, Mozart, Schubert, Hadyn and various Strausses over time, spy whatever paintings by Gustav Klimmt are currently on view, rehearse Orson Welles' cuckoo clock speech from *The Third Man* on the Riesenrad ferris wheel at Prater amusement park, and sit down for Sachertorte and whipped cream at the Sacher Hotel.

BEER VENUES

This part of Lower Austria is a wine-making region, with a tradition of communal drinking in Heuriger, or wine taverns. Beer drinkers must make do with brewpubs founded since the 1980s, or the new wave of craft beer bars. Look out for Pale Ales and Stouts from Bevog, Bierol, Brew Age and others, plus anything from Schremser.

▶ KÄNGURUH

🛈 🍴 Bürgerspittalgasse 20 - kaenguruh-pub.at - *shut Su; others from 17.00 - U3, U6 & S-bahn: Westbahnhof*

Well down its second decade, the city's best-groomed beer bar for grown-ups is a short walk from Westbahnhof. There is seating outside from April to September, and a dark wood interior year-round, candlelit as needs be. The list of up to 200 beers is strong on Austrian and Belgian, while the extensive menu includes everything but pudding.

▶ MEL'S DINER

🛈 🍴 Wipplingerstraße 9 - paddysco.at – *daily 11.00-02.00 – U3: Herrengasse*

The beeriest and most sophisticated of seven Irish-owned venues in Vienna is a

long beer hall that spills out onto the street in summer. Its draught beers tend to be obvious but behind these lie 200 mostly bottled beers from Austria and elsewhere, good enough to fill your week. Food is standard American diner with a few healthier options.

▶ BEAVER BREWING COMPANY

🛈 🍴 Liechtensteinstraße 69 – **beaverbrewing.at** – *Fr-Su from 12.00; Mo-Th from 16.30 – U6: Währinger St. Volsoper-Stadthalle, or tram 5: 33 Nußdorfer-Alserbachstraße Schönbrunnerstraße 98 – daily from 16.30 – U4: Margaretengürtel*

While COVID saw the city lose several beer bars this US-style brewpub next to Liechtenstein Palace Park spawned a second branch in Margareten. Each attracts a loyal ex-pat US community for its own brews and guests that have largely resisted the urge to haze, fruit, sugar or sour things up, and for their more authentic cut of burger and BBQ.

▶ HAWIDERE

🛈 🍴 Ullmannstraße 31 – **hawidere.at** – *daily 12.00-22.00 – U4, U6: Längenfeldgasse*

A short way out of the centre this 'Burger und Bier' place does what it says on the sign. Fourteen taps and a 40-strong bottled beer list manage to offer breadth without the geekery. The 'burgers' are excuses to put decent cooking between two bits of toasted bun, while the best things on the menu do not include the word 'burger' at all.

▶ AMMUTSØN

🛈 Barnabitengasse 10 – **ammutson.com** – *Sa-Su from 14.00; Mo-Fr from 16.00 – U3: Neubaugasse*

It is good occasionally to come across a bar where the most mainstream beer is a Porter from Dublin, the rest being an eclectic mix from small, independent breweries between Bucharest and Madrid. It styles itself a dive bar but the 80+ beers on a dozen taps and numerous shelves are way too classy for that. Food is cheese. Runs till 02.00 at least.

NEED TO KNOW

Austria is beautiful year-round, though the reasons vary. Vienna is not skiing country but rather a destination city. Its five-storey State Opera is delightfully and expensively absurd.

Accommodation: Hotels and apartments abound, at average European prices. There are regular deals at large, modern hotels next to Wien Hbf, which connects with the museum area (Karlsplatz), Cathedral (Stephansplatz), Danube canal (Schwedenplatz) and that ferris wheel (Prater).

Getting around: All trains, trams and buses within the city are covered by a Vienna Ticket (wienerlinien.at). A single ride costs €2.40; a day ticket to 01.00 next morning €5.80; 24 hours is €8; 48 hours €14.10; 72 hours €17.10; or the same for Monday midnight to 09.00 the following Monday.

Food: Viennese cuisine is influenced by German, with limitless pork, sauerkraut and mountains of potatoes, Italian for its pasta, tomatoes and all things dried, and Hungarian, bringing goulash and pickled vegetables. Portions are generally big and prices restrained. Breads and pastries abound, Healthier options are a popular novelty.

Hints: Tip by rounding up, adding between 5% and 15%. Jaywalking attracts a fine. Kissing, talking too loudly and eating smelly food will all risk you being ejected from public transport.

▶ BEERLOVERS

Gumpendorferstrasse 35 – beerlovers.at – shut Su; Sa 10.00-17.00; others 11.00-20.00 – U4: Kettenbrückengasse

One of Europe's most impressive beer shops stocks a range of 1,500 from nearly 30 countries in virtually every style, all clearly labelled. Making it up as you go along or by seeking inspiration won't work, so come with a list of must-haves and just try to improve on it. At the rear they have a tiny sampling area and operate a small brewery.

ABOUT WROCŁAW

- **Population:** 640,000
- **Local breweries:** Warsztat, Stu Mostow and Profesja.
- **Trains:** Wrocław Główny station is just off the centre and has a daily direct connection with Berlin (4.2 hours).
- **Airport:** Wrocław Copernicus airport is 13km W of the city and has direct connections with Stansted, Luton, Nottingham and Bristol. Bus 106 links it to Główny station every 15 minutes and takes 40-50 mins (PLN3.50 each way), while the more comfortable and direct WRO Airport Express (PLN8) leaves every 30 minutes and takes 35 minutes. Taxis cost roughly PLN60.
- **Currency:** Polish Złoty (PLN) 5.34 = £1

WROCŁAW

Say 'vrats-waff' in a cod Russian accent and you should get closer than most foreigners to pronouncing the name of the largest city in Lower Silesia, or southwest Poland. Until the First World War brought the end of the Austro-Hungarian Empire, this was German-speaking Breslau. Following the Second, those who spoke German were 'repatriated' to an equally devasted country that they did not know.

Today's successful, modern metropolis retains an impressive Old Town. One in five inhabitants is a student, which assists a beer culture that has become impressively broad, boosted by the annual Wrocław Good Beer Festival (see Beer Festivals and Events), regarded as the biggest and best in Poland.

Poles drink a lot of beer, mainly at home, averaging just under 100 litres a year – 50% more than the Brits and almost up there with their neighbours in Germany and the Czech Republic. The older generation drinks undemanding blond lagers, marginally better than UK brands but not as good as Czech Světlý or Munich Helles. Younger drinkers prefer the wheat beers, Pale Ales, Stouts, Porters among others.

Szczytnicki Park and the University's botanical gardens offer green space. If it's raining, Świebodzki station houses Kolejkowo, a huge model railway exhibition.

BEER VENUES

Poland will join the Euro at some point, though since 2016 the pleasingly named Złoty has been on the rise against both the Euro and Sterling. Despite this, the price of beer remains half that in the UK. Poland's 350+ small independent breweries make many styles but excel when it comes to Porters, Stouts and smoked beers, and make some decent Pale Ales. For lagers, stay Czech.

➤ SZYNKARNIA

🛈 🍴 Świętego Antoniego 15 – szynkarnia.com.pl
– Su 10.00-23.00; Mo-Th 16.00-24.00; Fr 15.00-02.00; Sa 10.00-02.00 – tram 3, 10, 14, 23, 33: Rynek

In a city full of good bars, this is my favourite. To the west of the Old Town, it looks like a large Welsh tearoom, has the vibe of an upmarket surfer's shack, serves scene-setting variants on pork and cheese, as well as stocking a great selection of Polish and imported draught and bottled beers. It is the epitome of cool, modern Poland.

▶ KONTYNUACJA

🍺🍴 Ofiar Oświęcimskichare 17
– kontynuacja.ontap.pl – *Sa-Su from 15.00; others from 16.00 – tram 3, 4, 10, 14, 23, 33: Świdnicka*

A couple of blocks south of the main square, this cutely sophisticated long bar sports 20 taps, including two handpulls, serving mostly Polish beers, plus collabs and tap takeovers. Classic Porters and Pale Ales outnumber the fruity stuff. They serve light bar snacks, and own a separate restaurant next door. Usually open till the small hours.

▶ 4 HOPS

🍺🍴 Ofiar Oświęcimskichare 46 – 4hops.pub – *Su-We 15.00-23.45; Th-Sa 15.00-01.00 – tram 2, 3, 4, 5, 6, 8, 10, 11, 17, 33: Galeria Dominikańska*

At the far end of the same street, a more obviously craft beer bar seems to attract all ages. Its cycling theme includes having some serious machines affixed firmly to the walls. Good service, light snacks and the sort of music that makes some of us feel young again, until we realise just how long ago it was first released.

▶ GRACIARNIA AND MARYNKA

🍺🍴 Kazimierza Wielkiego 39
– *tram 3, 4, 10, 14, 23, 33: Zamkowa*
Graciarnia: graciania.com.pl
– *daily from 12.00*
Marynka: FB/marynkapiwoiaperitivo
– *daily from 16.00*

On the out-of-town side of the inner ring road are two very different bars that share the same address, love of beer and passion for pizza. Graciarnia is a street corner pub with an old-fashioned design verging on elegance, carrying ±50 beers in total, while Marynka, the name of Poland's second most popular hop, is hidden behind the lobby of a neighbouring building, which leads to a courtyard and a much-vaulted, stone-floored, randomly furnished café. Here the beer offer is even broader.

▶ PINTA WROCŁAW

🍺🍴 Podwale 83 – pintawroclaw.pl – *daily 12.00-02.00 – tram 2, 3, 4, 5, 6, 8, 10, 11, 17, 33: Galeria Dominikańska*

The prolific Pinta brewery could and does claim to have begun the advance of craft beer in Poland, in 2011. A decade on it has followed BrewDog's lead in creating a pub

SZYNKARNIA

chain to showcase its own beers while encouraging others, as here. Snuck behind a large chain hotel, its layout shows its strength in hot weather. Offers burgers and alternatives.

▶ PIWNICA

⏣ Zaporoska 39e - FB/piwnika – *shut Su; Mo-Fr 11.00-21.00 – bus 126, 127, 144, 241, 249: Zaporoska*

The best place to buy Polish beers for take-home is this unassuming shop, 1km southwest of the main tourist area. It is filled to the gunnels with Polish craft beers and although visiting means taking a deliberate trip out by bus or taxi it will repay the effort.

GRACIARNIA

NEED TO KNOW

Wrocław is rated one of the easiest places to live in mainland Europe. For a sense of its history just wander round the Old Town and look up at the buildings, telling yourself stories made easy by their grandeur. The complex branching of the River Oder as it traverses the city has necessitated 100 bridges.

🛏 **Accommodation:** Seasons vary but even in summer bargains can be had, well below the European average. Try to stay in or near the much pedestrianised Old Town.

🚋 **Getting around:** With over 20 tram lines and almost 80 bus routes, the only place to find a map is online. A single journey costs PLN3.40, or PLN2.40 if you stick to one route and takes <15 minutes. A 24-hour ticket costs PLN11, 48-hour PLN20, 72- PLN26 and 168- PLN46. The overhead cable car in summer cuts the cross-town walk and is covered by regular tickets. Uber, Bolt and electric scooters are all well-established.

🍴 **Food:** If it is edible, the Poles will have at least three smoked versions of it, for different occasions. Pork is prominent and there are some good local cheeses. Cooking tends to be better in ethnic restaurants though standards generally are rising. The usual burger-pizza-craft triad is present too.

⭐ **Hints:** Tip 10% in restaurants or 15% if service is exceptional. No tip is expected in bars or hotels. Get used to using the translation apps.

WROCŁAW 163

INDEX

A
Amsterdam 36-41
   accommodation 41
   beer venues 37
   food 41
   getting around 41
   getting there 36

Antwerp 42-45
   accommodation 45
   beer venues 43
   food 45
   getting around 45
   getting there 42

Athens 46-47
   accommodation 47
   beer venues 47
   food 47
   getting around 47
   getting there 46

B
Bamberg 48-51
   accommodation 51
   beer venues 49
   food 51
   getting around 51
   getting there 48

Barcelona 52-55
   accommodation 55
   beer venues 53
   food 55
   getting around 55
   getting there 52

beer styles and
   brewing traditions 15

Berlin 56-61
   accommodation 61
   beer venues 57
   food 61
   getting around 61
   getting there 56

Bologna 62-65
   accommodation 65
   beer venues 63
   food 65
   getting around 65
   getting there 62

Bordeaux 66-69
   accommodation 69
   beer venues 67
   food 69
   getting around 69
   getting there 66

Bristol 70-73
   accommodation 73
   beer venues 71
   food 73
   getting around 73
   getting there 70

Brussels 74-79
   accommodation 79
   beer venues 75
   food 79
   getting around 79
   getting there 74

Budapest 80-83
   accommodation 83
   beer venues 81
   food 83
   getting around 83
   getting there 80

C
Copenhagen 84-87
   accommodation 87
   beer venues 85
   food 87
   getting around 87
   getting there 84

D
Dublin 88-91
   accommodation 91
   beer venues 89
   food 91
   getting around 91
   getting there 88

E
Edinburgh 92-95
   accommodation 95
   beer venues 93
   food 95
   getting around 95
   getting there 92

F
festivals and events 30
food 25

G
getting to and around
   Europe 9-13
      air 12
      bus 13
      planning the trip 9
      rail 9
      road 13
      sea 12

Gibraltar 96-97
   accommodation 97
   beer venues 97
   food 97
   getting around 97
   getting there 96

H I J K
Hamburg 98-101
   accommodation 101
   beer venues 99
   food 101
   getting around 101
   getting there 98

Helsinki 102-105
   accommodation 105

beer venues 103
food 105
getting around 105
getting there 102

L

Ljubljana 106-109
accommodation 109
beer venues 107
food 109
getting around 109
getting there 106
Luxembourg 110-111
accommodation 111
beer venues 111
food 111
getting around 111
getting there 110

M N

Madrid 112-115
accommodation 115
beer venues 113
food 115
getting around 115
getting there 112

O

Oslo 116-119
accommodation 119
beer venues 117
food 119
getting around 119
getting there 116

P Q

Paris 120-123
accommodation 123
beer venues 121
food 123
getting around 123
getting there 120

Porto 124-125
accommodation 125
beer venues 125
food 125
getting around 125
getting there 124
Prague 126-131
accommodation 131
beer venues 127
food 131
getting around 131
getting there 126
price of beer in Europe 36

R

Reykjavik 132-135
accommodation 135
beer venues 133
food 135
getting around 135
getting there 132
Riga 136-139
accommodation 139
beer venues 137
food 139
getting around 139
getting there 136
Rome 140-143
accommodation 143
beer venues 141
food 143
getting around 143
getting there 140

S

Stockholm 144-147
accommodation 147
beer venues 145
food 147
getting around 147
getting there 144

T U

Tallinn 148-151
accommodation 151
beer venues 149
food 151
getting around 151
getting there 148
Tel Aviv 152-155
accommodation 155
beer venues 153
food 155
getting around 155
getting there 152

V

Vienna 156-159
accommodation 159
beer venues 157
food 159
getting around 159
getting there 156

W X Y Z

Wrocław 160-163
accommodation 163
beer venues 161
food 163
getting around 163
getting there 160

CAMRA BOOKS

The Family Brewers of Britain
ROGER PROTZ

Britain's family brewers are stalwarts of beer making. Some date back as far as the 17th and 18th centuries and have survived the turbulence of world wars, bomb damage, recessions, floods, and the hostility of politicians and the temperance movement. This book, by leading beer writer Roger Protz, traces the fascinating and sometimes fractious histories of the families still running these breweries.

RRP **£25** Hardback   ISBN 978-1-85249-359-2
RRP **£17.99** Paperback   ISBN 978-1-85249-377-6

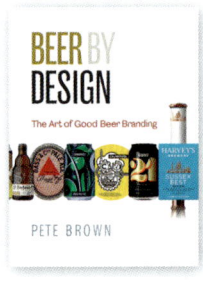

Beer by Design
PETE BROWN

The design of a beer label, pump clip, bottle or can has to do a lot of work to stand out, get noticed, and suggest to the thirsty punter that here is a beer they will enjoy. In this lavishly illustrated book, acclaimed beer writer Pete Brown traces the history of beer label design back to the UK's first-ever trade mark and beyond. He explores the conventions of successful beer design (and how they are now being shattered) and explains the tricks and secrets of successful design in a compelling and highly readable narrative.

RRP **£15.99**   ISBN 978-1-85249-368-4

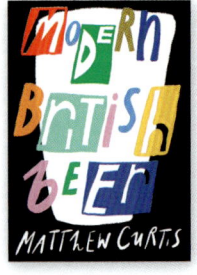

Modern British Beer
MATTHEW CURTIS

This book is about why modern British beer is important. Over the course of the past two decades the British beer scene as we know it has changed, forever. Matthew Curtis gives a personal insight into the eclectic and exciting world of modern British beer from a choice of 86 influential brews; from how they taste, how their ingredients are sourced, to the engaging stories of the people behind the scenes working hard to bring exciting beer to drinkers all over Britain. This book is a fantastic starting point to explore British beer with an exciting location closer than you think.

RRP **£15.99**   ISBN 978-1-85249-370-7

Modern British Cider
GABE COOK

Cider is one of the world's oldest drinks, with a heritage dating back at least 2,000 years. It formed an integral part of the landscape, economy and culture of many rural parts of the UK for centuries before being commoditised by industrial-scale production. Cider now faces a new change in the drinking landscape of Britain – the rise of craft drinks, which brings with it modern, discerning drinkers with different needs, habits and spending opportunities. Acclaimed cider expert Gabe Cook celebrates the heritage, diversity and innovation within the wonderful world of British cider today.

RRP **£15.99**   ISBN 978-1-85249-371-4

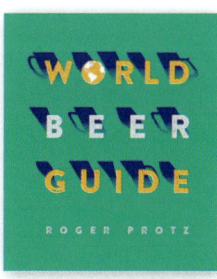

World Beer Guide
ROGER PROTZ

The world of beer is on fire. Traditional brewing countries are witnessing a spectacular growth in the number of beer makers while drinkers in such unlikely nations as France and Italy are moving from the grape to the grain. Drawing on decades of experience, Roger Protz takes readers on a journey of discovery around the world's favourite alcoholic drink – uncovering the interlinked stories behind the best breweries and beers across every continent in the world.

RRP **£30**   ISBN 978-1-85249-373-8

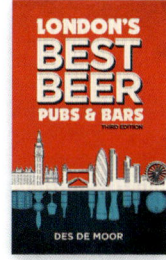

London's Best Beer, Pubs & Bars
3rd Edition
DES DE MOOR

The essential, indispensable and award-winning guide to one of the world's great beer cities is back with a fully revised and updated 3rd edition. From traditional pubs serving top-quality cask ale, to the latest on-trend bottle shop bars, and funky brewery taprooms in Victorian railway arches, London is now bursting with great beer and this book will direct you to the very best.

RRP **£16.99**   ISBN 978-1-85249-360-8

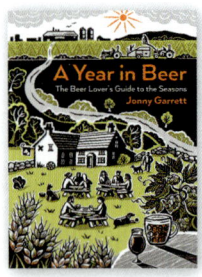

A Year in Beer
JONNY GARRETT

Chefs have been telling us to eat seasonally for decades, yet, when it comes to drink, we tend to reach for the same thing, whatever time of year. But beer is inextricably linked to the seasons, and thinking about it all seasonally opens the door to even greater beer experiences. *A Year in Beer* is an exploration of how our ingredients and tastes change with the seasons, and how Britain's rich brewing history still influences us today. Discover the best UK beer experiences, from summer beer festivals to the autumn hop and apple harvests — taking in the glory of the seasons that make them all possible.

RRP **£15.99** ISBN 978-1-85249-372-1

BOOKS FOR 2022

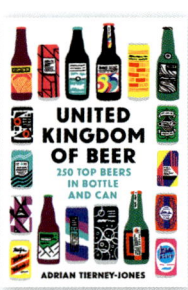

United Kingdom of Beer
ADRIAN TIERNEY-JONES

There is a thirst for good beer on these islands, a thirst for beer that satisfies the soul, quenches the thirst and leaves the drinker glowing with satisfaction. Whatever avenue your desire takes you down, whatever the occasion, be assured that there is a beer for you and acclaimed beer writer Adrian Tierney-Jones will help you make the right choice with his selection of 250 of the very best beers in bottle and can from around these islands.

RRP **£17.99** ISBN 978-1-85249-378-3

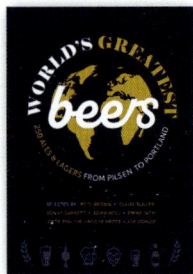

World's Greatest Beers
250 Ales & Lagers from Pilsen to Portland

Selected by: PETE BROWN, CLAIRE BULLEN, JONNY GARRETT, JOHN HOLL, EMMA INCH, LOTTE PEPLOW, ROGER PROTZ and JOE STANGE

This book is *the* definitive guide to the 250 best beers in the world today, selected by a panel of eight renowned international beer writers and influencers. Illustrated in full colour throughout, this high-quality book is a must-have for all self-respecting beer lovers.

RRP **£17.99** *August 2022* ISBN 978-1-85249-379-0

Order these and other CAMRA Books from **shop.camra.org.uk**